PRINCE OF PENZANCE

The Extraordinary 2015 Melbourne Cup

Published by Melbourne Books
Level 9, 100 Collins Street,
Melbourne, VIC 3000
Australia
www.melbournebooks.com.au
info@melbournebooks.com.au

National Library of Australia
Cataloguing-in-Publication entry
Author: Kristen Manning
Title: Prince Of Penzance: The Extraordinary 2015 Melbourne Cup
ISBN: 9781922129987 (paperback)
Subjects: Melbourne Cup (Horse race)
Prince of Penzance (Race horse)
Horse racing--Victoria--Melbourne.
Race horses--Victoria--Melbourne.
Dewey Number: 798.40099451

Front cover image: HISTORY AT FLEMINGTON! Prince Of Penzance and Michelle Payne win the 2015 Melbourne Cup. Photo courtesy of AAP Image/Julian Smith

Back cover image: THROUGH THE WAVES. Prince Of Penzance and Maddie Raymond at Warrnambool. Photo by Sharon Chapman

PRINCE OF PENZANCE

The Extraordinary 2015 Melbourne Cup

Kristen Manning

M

MELBOURNE BOOKS

For Ashley, who was so patient while Mum was writing her book for giants

CONTENTS

Foreword

FROM humble beginnings in 1861, the Melbourne Cup quickly developed into a race that captured the public's imagination. The first 154 renewals of the Melbourne Cup provided an amazing array of highlights featuring legendary names such as Phar Lap, Carbine, Peter Pan, Makybe Diva, Bart Cummings, Tommy Smith and Colin Hayes.

Each year brings a new remarkable story, but no running of the race in recent history entered the history books in such spectacular fashion as in 2015, when Michelle Payne became the first female jockey to ride a Melbourne Cup winner. Her win was a testament to her determination and talent. With a childhood dream to win the race, Michelle overcame tragedy and injury to deliver a racing fairytale.

Michelle's win highlighted thoroughbred racing's unique status as a sport where men and women compete against each other on a level playing field. Women continue to be increasingly well represented in the industry, and we hope that Michelle's trailblazing victory will encourage even more female participation across all areas of the sport.

The 2015 win was also special for other reasons. Champion trainer Darren Weir realised a long-held dream of his own to win the great race. Darren Weir's story is a brilliant example of grassroots country racing providing the nursery which produces future champions of the sport. From his country Victoria stables, Darren and his team produce countless winners, with the 2015 win in the Emirates Melbourne Cup by the tough six-year-old gelding Prince Of Penzance being the jewel in the crown.

The equal longest-priced winner in the history of the race, with odds at 100–1, Prince of Penzance courageously and spectacularly fought back from injury and illness to claim his place in history.

The 2015 Emirates Melbourne Cup typified exactly what the race is all about — determination, hard work and a race that can be won by horses from all over the globe or by one in our very backyard. It reminds us that it is important not to lose sight of your dreams.

The VRC is delighted that such an historic win in the Emirates Melbourne Cup has been documented in this wonderful tribute written by Kristen Manning, and I commend this book to all fellow lovers of racing.

Michael Burn
VRC Chairman

Prologue

MELBOURNE CUP DAY

TUESDAY, 3 November 2015 dawned cold and rough at Lady Bay Beach, Warrnambool. The waves attacked the sand, the grey skies threatened rain but didn't deliver. It was loud but quiet. Dramatic but serene.

Anyone watching from afar would expect to see little but squawking seagulls and the watery mist rising from the waves. If it was to be a head poking out of the water it would be that of a fish, or at a certain time of year, a whale.

But with a number of flourishing racing stables nearby, Lady Bay each morning hosts a procession of majestic thoroughbreds.

It was where Prince Of Penzance began his Melbourne Cup Day. He was already hard fit; there was not much more to do than get him to Flemington. But he was fresh and keen.

Being ridden off a pony up a small section of the 3.5-kilometre beach, he stretched his legs, he relaxed. He was ready to go.

As Prince Of Penzance returned to the stables, the sun rose. It remained crisp but it was a beautiful morning. One full of promise.

The horse picked at the remains of his breakfast of which he'd eaten half at around 4am. Around him his people prepared for the biggest day of his racing career. Not that he was particularly fussed;

he'd been on a float trip to the races twenty-three times before, and this day was no different.

Not a peep was heard from Prince Of Penzance on the 253-kilometre trip from Warrnambool to Flemington. So quiet is he when he travels that his strapper Maddie Raymond thinks he must be asleep.

But he knew when he had arrived. And he started to paw; he wanted to get out there. He wanted to be off and racing.

Part One

PRINCE OF PENZANCE

'We are going to have some fun with this horse.'

Chapter One

THE BEGINNING

THE Friday provincial race meeting is one of the quietest of the week.

Premiership jockeys are less likely to ride at them, and aside from a few local retirees the bulk of racegoers are owners … and the keenest ones at that. This included John Richards and Darren Lonsdale, who were the only two of Prince Of Penzance's owners to make the trek — John from Ballarat, Darren from Melbourne — to Stawell on 8 March 2013.

With just six rivals for his debut in a 1300-metre maiden, Prince Of Penzance was right in the market — second favourite behind the ironically named You Can't Beat Me.

It was hard for those on track to be confident however, John recalling that the young horse refused to behave. 'He played up badly. The worst I have ever seen.'

By this stage Prince Of Penzance had been gelded, his behaviour more to do with a lack of maturity. He was never particularly colty, Darren Weir said. 'John Foote told me that you have to geld the Pentires, so I took his advice.'

Fortunately, Prince Of Penzance put his excess energy into his race.

A little slowly away, Prince Of Penzance settled back, racing greenly (racing speak for a horse running a bit erratically due to a lack of experience) but picking himself up and charging late to overhaul the leader.

'Prince Of Penzance is running him down in a hurry, and he's got there,' said the race caller.

It was not the first time Michelle Payne had been aboard the immature bay. She knew from track work and jump-outs that he was promising, but by winning at debut at a distance that was to be far short of his best, he gave her cause for some excitement.

'He is really green, but he surprised me how he really picked up,' she told the horse's connections.

Darren Weir was also impressed, though it was still very early days. 'I knew at this stage that he had ability … but not how much.'

And so Prince Of Penzance had won his first $9000.

Members of the Wilawl Go Racing syndicate watched from their various workplaces on their mobiles, dismayed when the broadcast dropped out. There was no vision until the 600 metres, but soon they were all yelling at their phones, jumping up and down, ringing each other. Michael Wilson had been ill, so much so that he didn't really take it all in, and was soon in hospital on a drip. It was not till a week later that he recovered sufficiently to watch the replay. And then he watched again. And again.

Seventeen days later over 1350 metres at Donald, rising in class, Prince Of Penzance was 10–1, bookmakers and punters all aware that it is not the easiest of tasks for a horse to step up from a maiden to win again.

Darren Weir had Taiyoo, a more favoured runner in the same race, a horse who had also won his first start but by a bigger margin. He was to jump from the inside barrier, Prince Of Penzance had drawn out wide.

All bar one of the Wilawl Go Racing crew were on course, excited. 'Now you know it is hard to win second up,' Neil Laws warned, but Andrew Wilson was more confident: 'I think we have a special horse; he can do it.'

While Taiyoo sat third behind a tearaway leader, Prince Of

Penzance was out the back, spotting his rivals over ten lengths. As his stablemate made a winning run, Prince Of Penzance was checked by a broken-down horse at the turn, the sort of interference that would put most young, inexperienced horses out of business.

But not Prince Of Penzance — he just kept going, hooking out wide and finishing off strongly to finish third. He was beaten a bit less than three lengths by Taiyoo, who would also go on to prove himself a high-class performer, winning at Group Three and Listed level, and only just missing out on an Adelaide Cup victory.

So eye-catching was Prince Of Penzance's run that seventeen days later he was favourite stepping up to 1600 metres at Ballarat, his home track.

It was a weekday, hard for owners to get to, but Andrew and Michael Wilson finished work early and headed to the track. Soon noticing a bias favouring horses on pace, they were a little concerned, but the stable had also taken note and it looked a nice chance to see how Prince Of Penzance would fare closer up in running. And it would be a good learning experience for him.

Despite drawing another tricky wide gate, he was fast enough out of the barriers to take the lead. By the time he got to the home turn he was a couple of lengths in front.

'Michelle gave him a little squeeze and he gave a bit more, and won easily,' Andrew recalled, laughing at the memory of becoming the sort of excitable and vocal owners who everyone else notices … lots of yelling and fist-pumping. 'I remember hitting my race book so hard against my hand that it sounded like a whip cracking.'

Prince Of Penzance was again green, drifting out a bit late, but he held a two-length margin to the line and was now the winner of two of his first three starts, Michelle Payne noting that 'he has still got a bit to learn, but he is a really nice horse'.

Darren Weir, with a cheeky grin on his face, turned to the Wilsons, saying, 'Boys, we are going to have some fun with this horse.'

Chapter Two

TO TOWN

THE next step for Prince Of Penzance was a tougher one. Not only did he have to run another 200 metres, but he was taking on city-class performers, heading to town for the first time in a $100,000 1800-metre contest at Caulfield.

While his country form was impressive, this was a much more difficult task and he was double-figure odds. Owner Andrew Broadfoot remembers having a nice bet, thinking 'he might never be this sort of price again'.

And it was the day that the stable decided to add some arsenal: Prince Of Penzance was to wear blinkers for the first time.

With his peripheral vision, the horse is bombarded with a multitude of sights as he races, a blur of light and colour. It is bound to detract from their concentration, especially if the horse is inexperienced.

Part of a hood fitted over the horse's head, blinkers curve around the back of the eye and forward, restricting the wearer's view so that he can see only straight ahead. Which is where the finishing line is.

Prince Of Penzance's first metropolitan run was not a winning one, but it was one that earned him plenty of fans. A little slowly away from an inside gate, he sat midfield around nine lengths from the leaders.

Into the clear straightening he gathered momentum, running on strongly to be beaten by the barest of margins. He went into many a punter's black book that day, with a Best Bets commentator noting 'nice horse, follow!'

'What a run,' Darren Weir said to owner Pam Wilson, who had watched the race with him.

The Men In Hats Syndicate's Sam Brown remembers the day well. He had just completed the twenty-four-hour Oxfam Trailwalker challenge and was tired — well, exhausted. He had not slept more than an hour, but there was 'no way' he was missing his horse's first city race.

Popping a couple of No-Doz tablets to ensure he was alert enough to enjoy the race he headed out to Caulfield, glad he made the effort.

'He absolutely flew home to just miss out in a photo finish. Wow, how good was that, what an experience! We knew we had a horse worthy of city class.'

And it was a pretty exciting day to have a runner, that day chosen by the Melbourne Racing Club to farewell the unbeaten champion, Black Caviar.

'It was a special day,' Andrew Wilson recalled, 'one I will never forget. People were standing four and five deep while she paraded. She stopped for pats and photos, I couldn't believe how calm she was.'

Everyone's focus was, of course, on Black Caviar. The bay gelding at one stage walking in front of her in the pre-parade ring was barely noticed. Except by his proud owners, who observed how calmly he walked among the throng. 'He took everything in his stride,' said Andrew.

Not surprisingly, years later one of Andrew's prized possessions is a photograph he took that day, a sprinting star in the background and a future Melbourne Cup winner ahead of her.

Two weeks later, Prince Of Penzance experienced the wide open spaces of Flemington for the first time. And he liked them, though he was rather a naughty boy during the running of the Flemington Green Fields Handicap.

Again a little tardy out of the gates, Prince Of Penzance refused to settle. Horses usually respond well to Michelle Payne's gentle hands, but on this day she was given a difficult ride. He pulled, both hard and long. For most of the race.

A horse expends a lot of extra energy pulling — their mouth opens, their head goes up. This is energy required to fight out the race. Usually after racing in such a way, a horse will be under pressure a fair way from home, they will drop out of contention early and finish at the tail of the field.

But Prince Of Penzance was having none of that. Instead of going backwards as could be expected, he was charging forward. Reeling in the leader, putting his nose out on the line. A Flemington winner in his very first racing campaign at just his fifth start.

'That just shows what a serious horse he is,' Michelle Payne told the press, those left to report on the final race of the day. 'Not many horses can pull like that, and throw their head in the air, and still attack the line the way he did.'

'I think he has got a really bright future,' she added. 'I hope I can stick with him.'

Darren Weir could not quite believe what he saw that day, noting that 'he looked to do a lot wrong … he got into a terrible rhythm. But once Michelle was able to get him clear he stretched out well.'

So why is this horse so inclined to pull? 'That's just him,' said Darren, 'he is a bit of a dag, still young in the head.'

A big group of joyous owners welcomed Prince Of Penzance back to scale. It was, said Sam Brown, 'a dream come true, a city winner'.

'And it was not just us guys who were excited; our wives and girlfriends had jumped on board too. They were hooked! We celebrated long and hard, and it was great meeting a lot of the other owners, most of whom were also celebrating their first city winner.'

This was including Darren Lonsdale, who was grateful to his co-owners for letting him, as a first-time owner, accept the trophy.

'Just accepting that was like winning the Melbourne Cup,' he joked.

Sam Brown well remembers something Michelle Payne said that day, something so stunning he thought he had misheard her: 'This is probably the best horse I have ridden.'

It was not so long ago that the congratulations to owners came pretty much to an end once they'd left the racetrack. But now social media keeps the excitement going, and Andrew Wilson enjoyed watching the ongoing discussions of his horse's big win.

'Well done Michelle! I listened from Hong Kong, excited and happy. Go The Prince!' Michael Wilson said on Twitter.

'Massive win, good job Michelle Payne, tough horse,' said former jockey Sam Hyland.

And Michelle replied, 'He's pretty good, horses just don't do that ... Melbourne Cup horse.'

At the time the Group One Queensland Derby, contested over 2400 metres at sunny Eagle Farm in June, was on the radar, but Darren was expressing concerns.

'He couldn't race like that in a Queensland Derby and expect to run well,' he said. 'He has got the ability, but I am not sure he has got the mental attitude yet.'

A decision of whether or not Prince Of Penzance would head north was, however, made for them, the horse pulling up sore after the Flemington run. Surgery was required, Prince Of Penzance having to make what would be the first of four trips to the Ballarat Veterinary Practice's Equine Clinic.

'After the excitement of his first city win we were brought back to earth pretty quickly,' Sam Brown said. 'The rollercoaster emotions of horse racing ... we knew we had a talented horse, but we were worried that he may not come back the same.'

On 14 May, Prince Of Penzance went under the knife of Dr Brian Anderson, who removed from his off fore fetlock an osteochondral fragment, better known as a bone chip. It was arthroscopic surgery, often referred to as keyhole surgery.

Typically, a rest period of three to four months is recommended. While Prince Of Penzance was recuperating plans were being made for him to undertake his future training at Warrnambool, where access to sand and water would help him in his comeback.

In the meantime his owners had watched as his form was tested at stakes level for the first time, when Wowee, who had finished tenth behind Prince Of Penzance at Flemington, at her next start won the Group Three South Australian Oaks at Morphettville.

Chapter Three

THE FIRST COMEBACK

SEVEN months after his first operation, having trialled nicely at Camperdown with Michelle aboard, Prince Of Penzance resumed in a 1410-metre contest at Flemington.

It was not an easy race for Michelle. Prince Of Penzance was caught wide throughout, finishing an unspectacular but solid seventh. The winner of the race was Sistine Demon, who Michelle had ridden to Donald and Moonee Valley victories at her two previous starts.

She'd had the choice of rides — she chose her boy.

And while on the day it must've hurt a little, her decision was quickly endorsed, Prince Of Penzance two weeks later stepping up to 1600 metres at Moonee Valley where, as favourite, he recorded his fourth and easiest win to date.

Joining in at the turn from midfield, Prince Of Penzance quickly rounded up his rivals, racing away by 2 3/4 lengths.

'Prince Of Penzance is coming on very strongly,' called the course broadcaster. 'Here comes the Prince, he said see you later boys!'

'He tracked into the race beautifully,' Michelle Payne reported, 'and he really hit the line well.'

'He is a really nice progressive sort of horse,' said Darren Weir, telling reporters that summer features, such as the Mornington Cup, were on the agenda.

Deane Lester, on the following morning's *Correct Weight* show on RSN radio, said that 'probably the most impressive winner of the day was Prince Of Penzance'.

Beaten but hardly disgraced when second as equal favourite over 1720 metres at his next start at Flemington, Prince Of Penzance got well back off a slow start, finishing off nicely.

Next came Prince Of Penzance's first crack at a stakes race, the Listed Mornington Cup Prelude that in previous years had been run as the Victoria Gold Cup.

Contested over 2000 metres at Caulfield, the race attracted a field of eleven, with the Gai Waterhouse trained Laidback Larry, who had won four in a row, a hot odds-on favourite.

Prince Of Penzance's owners were excited, though brought back to earth a little when in the race before his the lightly raced filly Kiss A Rose collapsed and died in the mounting yard, most likely from heart failure.

'We just thought about those owners,' Sam Brown said, 'how shattering it was, how much grief they must have been feeling. My motto had always been to celebrate every win like it is your last. You never know what is around the corner in this game.'

Settling around midfield along the rails in the $120,000 race, Prince Of Penzance was at times a little keen, with the favourite getting his own way in front. There is a danger, in slowly run races, of horses getting caught up in the ruck, but Michelle had her horse sliding away from the fence in plenty of time.

Approaching the turn Prince Of Penzance was putting himself into the race, and a vocal group of owners watching from the mounting yard began to scream, 'Go Prince, c'mon Prince, this is your chance!'

At the 300 metres he was third, with Oregon Spirit on his outside who for a few strides appeared to be travelling a little better. At the 200 metres the pair began to draw clear. For a hundred exciting, nail-biting metres it was a battle between two determined horses.

But it was Prince Of Penzance who most wanted the win. From

the 100 metres he got away from his rivals, and as he crossed the line a 3/4 length in front, racegoers got a taste of how this horse's owners could celebrate … loudly and enthusiastically!

'A Listed win — we thought that was the achievement of a horse's lifetime,' enthused Andrew Broadfoot.

Michelle was beaming, her faith in the horse justified. 'Right from the start he showed me that he had above-average ability, and he just keeps showing it at every start.'

'He won in good fashion,' Darren Weir said. 'He is starting to put it together now. He did a few things wrong, but he is not over-racing as badly as he used to. He has had a couple of runs at 2000 metres now and won them both. Hopefully when he gets to a mile and a half he will be even better.'

Prince Of Penzance's owners celebrated that night, their pride and joy was now a stakes winner. Sam Brown remembers being out late with Arthur Rickard and Darren Lonsdale, trophy in hand.

'After a few bottles of red in celebration we sent Arthur home in the back of the taxi with the trophy. We laughed so hard when a message came in the next morning from the Weir stable; "Does anyone know the whereabouts of the trophy?"'

The next morning Prince Of Penzance was discussed on RSN radio, again on the *Correct Weight* show. 'He is a beauty,' said Warren Huntly, 'it was a terrific win from a really promising horse.' Deane Lester agreed, noting that 'he is a young up-and-comer who looks as though the further he goes the better he will be'.

A couple of options awaited Prince Of Penzance: the Mornington Cup and the Launceston Cup. Darren Weir could see the benefits of both, a trip interstate likely to 'make him grow up a bit, flying there and staying in a different stable'.

'But the Mornington Cup gives you free entry into the Caulfield Cup, so we will need to sit down and think seriously about it.'

In the back of Darren's mind was the fact that he had never enjoyed the best of times at Mornington … 'I just don't have any luck there; my horses just don't seem to race well there for some reason.'

Nevertheless, the Mornington Cup was chosen as Prince Of Penzance's next assignment, with connections looking forward to seeing what he could do stepping up to 2400 metres for the first time.

A big crowd was in attendance, Michael Wilson a bit in awe — 'How's this,' he said to his fellow owners, 'all these people coming here today to see our horse race!'

The owners took their place in the grandstand. John Richards at the time was having troubles with his eyes and struggled to see. David Wilson sitting next to him described the race: 'He's in front, he's in with a chance.'

However, Prince Of Penzance had again wanted to race a little keenly and this was harder to get away with in a longer race. He had hit the lead, and while others were able to catch him late he fought on strongly to finish fourth, beaten less than a length.

While he was game, connections could not help but feel a little discouraged. His lead up form had been great, he was a short 2–1 favourite. 'I have never seen Weiry so disappointed,' Sam Brown recalled, adding that, 'we hated being favourite; there was so much pressure, so much expectation.'

Another Listed race was next for Prince Of Penzance: the Roy Higgins Quality, run over 2600 metres at Flemington in honour of one of the country's finest ever jockeys.

Again favourite, Prince Of Penzance sat third-last and ran on well, the winner Cooldini having enjoyed the advantage of being closer up during the running.

A couple of weeks later, Prince Of Penzance was again sore and back to Ballarat, Dr Ian Fulton performing surgery on both front fetlocks, bone chips again the issue.

Another period of recuperation followed and again connections had to wonder if their champ would make it back … and if he did, would he be the same horse?

He did not take long to answer that question.

Chapter Four

THE MOONEE VALLEY CUP

JUST under six months later several of Prince Of Penzance's owners journeyed all the way to St Arnaud to watch him compete in a jump-out (Arthur Rickard was so keen to get there after getting lost en-route that he incurred a speeding fine), Darren Lonsdale recording their banter on his phone after the horse had finished off gamely.

'He travelled really nicely, he is really settling well now,' Michelle Payne said.

'But he still looks to be full of himself,' said John Richards.

'He is, but once he gets out onto the track he settles down beautifully,' Michelle replied, adding that for a couple of strides he was left a little flat-footed as the speed went on.

But his final effort was strong — 'He was flying through the line.'

'Are you going to ride him in the Melbourne Cup?' John joked. 'We will give you an extra twenty bucks for that.'

They laughed about a crack at the Cox Plate as well. 'That's a bit greedy,' Michelle laughed. 'You might be up for both races,' said Arthur's daughter Jenny Monks, 'but will the horse?'

'We will find out. It's all looking good so far.'

A couple of weeks later, Prince Of Penzance battled on gamely to finish eighth in a 1400-metre handicap at Caulfield.

Taking a little longer than usual to come fully to hand, Prince Of Penzance was out of the placings at his next two starts at Flemington and Caulfield, but both races were run at a slow pace, making it hard for horses from back in the field to make up ground.

The Caulfield eighth nearly ten lengths from the winner was, however, a disappointment. Connections stood in the mounting yard for some time after the horses had left. Darren Weir was scratching his head. The replay was watched and analysed, but it gave no answers.

'It doesn't matter how many times you watch it, it was a shocker,' Darren said.

Had injury and surgery taken its toll? Had they seen the best of their horse? Darren was dejected, but not beaten. And a plan was hatched: the horse would race on a track with more cushion.

And so he headed to Gippsland for the 2050 metres of the Moe Cup in mid-October. Darren was running late, rushing into the yard in time to help the strapper apply the horse's tongue tie (a strip of cloth, often stockings, passed through the mouth to prevent a horse getting his tongue over the bit). Prince Of Penzance, whose interest had been piqued by a session of schooling (jumping) over logs that morning, was keen to go and in the process bit his trainer's finger.

But any pain felt by Darren was soon forgiven, for it was in that race that Prince Of Penzance showed a glimpse of his true form with the blinkers reapplied. He was up to his old tricks, over-racing, putting his head up. But he was strong to the line, a close second. Dreams were back on track.

The Moonee Valley Cup is not the main race held at Moonee Valley on the last Saturday each October. That honour of course belongs to the W. S. Cox Plate, Australia's most prestigious weight-for-age contest.

It does, however, well and truly predate the Cox Plate, that race first run in 1922, while the Cup has been contested since 1883. The day was for many years referred to as the Gold Cup meeting, and even when Phar Lap won his first Cox Plate in 1930 the main headlines in the press belonged to Shadow King, who had won the longer race.

And so Prince Of Penzance was partaking in history when taking his place in the 2014 Moonee Valley Cup, run at Group Two level with a value of $250,000.

His owners were thrilled to be a part of one of Australia's biggest race days, Sam Brown recalling that they were 'over the moon'.

'We had been to Cox Plates before, mainly in the public boozing and belting out "The Horses" along with Daryl Braithwaite. Now here we were with a runner. He wasn't much fancied in betting so we went along feeling no pressure. We just wanted to enjoy the day as we thought it was a once-in-a-lifetime event.'

Not bustled having drawn the outside gate of nine, Prince Of Penzance settled last. It is not the ideal place to be at the tight turning track that is Moonee Valley. Crowding can take place and those out wider enjoy the benefit of the cambered turn.

And so Michelle had to ride for luck.

Though Prince Of Penzance is the sort of horse who makes his own luck. When a tight run presented itself with 400 metres to go, he took it. By the time the field straightened for home he was third, and then he was off and away, saluting by 1 1/4 lengths and giving New Zealanders a reason to be proud as he left a couple of imported gallopers — the German-bred Le Roi and the Irish-bred Au Revoir — in his wake.

Interviewed on horseback by Sam Hyland as she returned to scale, Michelle was delighted. And so proud of her horse's effort.

'Geez, it was tight coming around the corner, but he just burst through there and he was flying through the line.

'The first corner he got a little bit keen, but he began too slowly to ride him forward, which was the original plan. So I just had to go to Plan B, which was to get him to settle. Once he got into the rhythm he was beautiful.

'I thought I'll just have to ride for luck now, we can't go around them and win. It is just fantastic. This is one of my favourite days of racing, I am so happy to be a winner.'

Darren Weir admitted to being a little concerned during the race — 'I didn't know what to be thinking but that's where she rides best, full credit to her. It was a great ride, she was very patient. And the horse was terrific.'

Television cameras swung to the owners. Neil Laws' raw emotion overtook him, his obvious glee making him an overnight sensation as his wild celebrations went viral on You Tube.

Men In Hats Syndicate member Mike Botting was grabbed to do an interview, journalist Bruce Clark having a laugh with him about the owners being dressed up in the purple, white and green of Prince Of Penzance's silks.

'That's what we've invested our winnings on,' Mike joked. 'We've got ties, cufflinks, scarves ... we might have suits by next time!'

'His best win so far,' said another delighted owner, Bruce Dalton. 'A lot of blokes go through their whole life without getting a horse like this. He hasn't won a Group One, but he still has a couple of years left.'

Sam Brown 'couldn't believe' they'd won, that Prince Of Penzance's name was on an honour roll along with the likes of Melbourne Cup winners Americain and Kingston Rule: 'Fancy that, his name was now etched in history.'

A two-kilogram penalty for the win saw Prince Of Penzance make his way up in the order of entry for the Melbourne Cup, and it was still a possibility. But he had pulled a couple of shoes off during the Moonee Valley Cup, and his feet were a little sore. He would not be 100 percent for the Tuesday.

Two weeks later Prince Of Penzance returned to Flemington, the Group Two Queen Elizabeth Stakes his next assignment. For the first time Michelle Payne was not aboard, unable to take the ride due to suspension. Sydney jockey Hugh Bowman took her place. He had the horse nicely placed, but the combination of top weight of 58 kilograms and too firm a track proved a stumbling block — though he was still a courageous second.

The day was a special one for the Men In Hats crew who had long been fans of Hugh Bowman. In March 2010, syndicate member Scott Jenke had celebrated his buck's party at a Warwick Farm race meeting, and while many of the revellers were not in a fit state to notice the last race, Scott's brother Paul and Sam Brown had done the form and put a quadrella on.

Alive in the last of the four legs it was a Hugh Bowman mount who won them a nice dividend. Sam remembers he and Paul jumping up and down on the fence, yelling to the jockey, 'Give us your goggles!'

'Hugh magnificently obliged and instantly elevated himself to legend status in our eyes. He has always been and will always be one of my favourite jockeys, and he was riding our horse!'

Of course, Michelle is also a great favourite, and it was unusual for Prince Of Penzance's owners not to be talking to her before a race.

'I couldn't resist having a cheeky dig,' Sam recalled, saying, 'Hey Hugh, where are your pearl earrings?'

Prince Of Penzance was again in the placings in the Group Two Sandown Classic, with Michelle back in the saddle at his next outing. Racing a touch keenly early, he was badly held up for runs at the turn, getting into the clear and boxing on well to the line to finish a close-up third.

That effort was all the more meritorious when he was later found to be sore. Another bone chip, again on that troublesome off fore, was located and removed.

A well-earned break was to be enjoyed, Prince Of Penzance settling in nicely at Laura Dixon's Dowling View Equine Centre.

Already at this time betting was open for the following year's Melbourne Cup. Generous odds were on offer and Andrew Broadfoot was one to have a dabble. The day after he had a bet his phone rang.

Prince Of Penzance was ill, dangerously ill.

Chapter Five

LIFE OR DEATH

IT was fortunate on that otherwise normal afternoon in late January, eight weeks or so after Prince Of Penzance's operation, that Laura Dixon was at home. The owner and manager of Dowling View Equine Centre was preparing to move a delivery of sand when she noticed that the bay looked a bit agitated.

But just a little, as though a fly or something minor was annoying him. Then he got down and rolled, kicking out a bit. Laura thought it might be his rug that was proving an irritation, so she removed it.

Some would've left it at that. Fortunately, Laura was both diligent and caring.

And so she kept watch and when Prince Of Penzance continued to roll, Laura called Darren Weir. Already she had erred on the side of caution by ringing the stable vet, but he was on the other side of Ballarat at the time.

During the next five minutes Laura witnessed what all lovers of horses dread. Prince Of Penzance was no longer just rolling, he was throwing himself on the ground. He was in pain.

Within ten minutes Dr Nicola Lynch was on the scene, but it proved difficult for her to inspect her patient — he was under too much stress to stand still. It took three lots of drugs before she could even get near him.

Getting him onto the float proved difficult, taking all of Laura's and Dr Lynch's patience and equine expertise. And once in he again wanted to go down.

Fortunately the equine clinic was close by, just a quick trip around the corner, at the back of Ballarat race course. Specialist surgeon Dr Brian Anderson and his team — a nurse, an anaesthetist and an assistant — had everything set up and ready to go.

All up it was just an hour from Prince Of Penzance's first symptoms of colic to him being under the knife.

Dr Anderson well remembers Prince Of Penzance's arrival at the clinic, and things looked bleak. 'He was not in good shape,' he said, shaking his head. 'He was in a lot of pain and had not responded to several pain-killing injections.'

The normal heart rate of the thoroughbred at rest sits at around 36–42 beats per minute. At this stage, Prince Of Penzance's was soaring into the eighties and nineties.

The lack of response to pain relief, Dr Anderson says, is the first sign of danger, with ninety percent of colic (a generic term for a stomach upset) cases rectified by a single dose.

'It is a bit like a person having an upset stomach after a curry — you take a panadol and lie down and usually you are fine within the hour.'

But in the other ten percent of cases, something more serious occurs. The digestive gases build up and the abdomen begins to distend. And this is what was happening to the now very uncomfortable and distressed Prince Of Penzance.

It was, said Dr Anderson 'a life or death situation'.

After a couple of diagnostic tests, an ultrasound and a rectal exam to see what was going on, Prince Of Penzance was prepared for surgery. He was placed in a confined area next to a shifting partition.

Within five minutes, once the initial dose of anaesthetic had kicked in, he went down. The moving wall was gently lowered, the horse slid across to an awaiting water bed warmed to a comfortable thirty-seven degrees.

From there he was hooked up to a ventilator and an anaesthetic machine, turned upside down and transported to the adjoining surgery by a pulley system. And then Dr Anderson went to work, beginning with a forty-centimetre incision through the horse's stomach. 'A bit like opening your jacket,' he said as he deftly unzipped his coat.

Sometimes what confronts the equine surgeon at this stage is distressing. The 'large and long' intestines (in the horse the small intestines measure at around eighteen metres in length, the large intestines about six) in reaction to the build up of gases start to twist, cutting off blood supply. It can take only a couple of hours for irreversible damage to occur. Tissues starved of oxygen begin to die.

Parts of the intestine can be removed, the remaining parts joined, as Dr Anderson put it, 'a bit of plumbing'.

When this occurs the likelihood of complete recovery plummets, from a seventy to eighty percent chance, to fifty percent or less.

Fortunately, thanks to the speed in which Prince Of Penzance made it to the clinic, in this case there was not yet any major damage.

And so, over the course of a couple of hours, a twist of the large intestine was fixed. It is work of high concentration, with little margin for error. The skill and experience of the surgeon kicks in.

After being sewn back up, Prince Of Penzance was placed back on the pulley and moved to the nearby recovery room. This is another crucial stage.

Anaesthetic suppresses normal function, and horses are not made to lie down for prolonged periods. Neither are they made for deep sleep. They are creatures of flight and their first instinct when something concerns them is to run.

And of course waking up in a strange environment, feeling groggy and a bit sore, a horse will worry. Or worse still, panic. The recovery room is therefore heavily padded, just in case a horse begins to thrash out.

Such was the case with the legendary American filly Ruffian, who, having been successfully operated on after breaking down in her famous match race with Foolish Pleasure (her only defeat), awoke from her anaesthesia in a frenzy, injuring herself so severely that she had to be euthanised.

It is rare, said Dr Anderson, for a high-class horse to react in such a way. He has found that the better the horse, the more likely they are to stay calm; they have an internal strength, an intelligence that better prepares them for the unknown.

'Champions,' he explains, 'are strong and tough. And they know they are special; they have that arrogance, a swagger, a confidence.'

Prince Of Penzance is one such horse. From him there was no panic, no kicking out. He rose slowly, gingerly, looking after himself. Just four hours after he felt those first worrying twinges of pain he was in recovery, being closely monitored.

It was not long afterwards that Prince Of Penzance gave hospital staff some cause for concern. He did not look happy; he was pawing at the ground.

And so they rushed to his side. But this tough, hardy thoroughbred was not in pain. He was hungry!

This is one of the very best signs that a horse has come through an operation well. With the intestines needing time to recover, the patient is not fed for at least twenty-four hours, and the first offering of a couple of handfuls of chaff is either rejected or gratefully received. When it is the latter, the horse is on his way to recovery. When he is ready for a snack, says Dr Anderson, you know he is going well.

He is, by no means, out of the woods. This particular type of surgery is demanding on the equine body. After an operation for bone chips a horse can lose around five, maybe ten kilograms. After a procedure to relieve colic they can shed up to fifty kilograms, around ten percent of their entire body weight.

Full recovery is a slow process, the horse regaining weight at the rate of around one kilogram a day. It takes three months for the horse to regain sufficient strength to be ridden, and once a horse suffers from a severe colic attack they are at risk of recurrence.

The threat is at its highest within the first three months, and decreases a little more after a year, all the more so after three years.

Darren Weir knows all about this, for in 2002, the year before she finished second in the first of Makybe Diva's three historic Melbourne Cup victories, his gallant mare She's Archie had twice been struck.

And it was the team at Ballarat who saved her life also, Dr Anderson performing both procedures. 'We joke with Darren that we should operate on all his Melbourne Cup aspirants!'

Prince Of Penzance remained at the equine clinic for a week, followed by three weeks in a box, another three in a small yard and six in his paddock.

He recovered well, though it was not completely smooth sailing, with the incision site contracting an infection and a course of antibiotics required. And then, despite Laura Dixon's and Darren Weir's best efforts in choosing just the right companion for Prince Of Penzance, his paddock mate kicked him and he ended up with a massive haematoma … 'a basketball on his hind leg'.

Fortunately, another week in the box saw Prince Of Penzance fully recovered from that setback, and the rest of his spell was bother-free. Nobody could have foreseen that just nine months later the horse would run the race of his life.

Chapter Six

THE SPRING

SELDOM have owners been as happy to run eighth as were the Prince Of Penzance group upon his return to racing in the Memsie Stakes at Caulfield on Saturday, 29 August 2015.

It had been just over nine months since he last raced, eight since his third operation for bone chips and seven since his life-threatening colic attack.

Getting back to the races was quite the achievement in itself. Running well, many felt, would be a miracle. Especially as it was his first crack at Group One company.

For the first time in his career Prince Of Penzance was triple figure odds, 100–1. Settling back from a wide gate, he hooked out at the 600 metres and started to make up ground. He didn't pick up all of his well-credentialled rivals, but enough of them. A most encouraging effort, finishing ahead of such outstanding gallopers as Happy Trails, Dandino and Fawkner, beaten only 2 1/4 lengths, recording the second fastest final 400 metres.

'Prince Of Penzance has run out of his skin,' said race caller Greg Miles.

Michelle Payne was delighted, telling owners that, 'He began really nicely, and just came back and settled beautifully. The speed was nice and genuine for the first half and they steadied mid-race, which gave him the chance to tack on. He got a lovely cart up behind Weary, which took us right into the straight.

'He just wanted to lay in a fraction when I first went with him, so I pulled the stick in the left hand. He straightened up beautifully and was really good to the line and really good through the line. It was a perfect first up run.'

His owners were relieved and happy, slapping each other on the back. Pam and David Wilson had a wedding to go to but had sat out in their car to listen, enjoying updates from Michael. They were happy from afar.

Sixty-two kilograms made Prince Of Penzance's second up task in the Gold Nugget at Ballarat a tough one, but he was a sound fifth carrying eight kilograms more than the winner, Freshwater Storm.

'It looked a strange decision at the time to run a Melbourne Cup contender at Ballarat,' said part-owner John Richards.

The metropolitan tracks at the time, he explained, were being prepared firm, too hard for Prince Of Penzance and his troublesome fetlocks. Michelle Payne phoned city track curators to see if the courses were to be watered … they were not.

'We did not want to expend the horse and the Ballarat track was in good order, so it's there we went.'

It is not every day that a Ballarat race features in a story in the *Gold Coast Bulletin* but this one did, touted as a bit of a match race. Owner Stephen Wilson works for the Gold Coast Suns and the team's captain Gary Ablett had Baron Archer in the same race. While neither horse saluted, Stephen won bragging rights, his horse fifth, Gary Ablett's seventh.

The Group Three JRA Cup at Moonee Valley was next, and after covering ground behind all the way winner Escado he was fifth less than two lengths away.

'I was really happy with the Prince's performance today,' Michelle Payne reported. 'He got into a nice position and travelled well. I was happy with how he raced, his racing manners. He put in a nice first

600 metres and then the speed really went on and got him off the bit, but he was really strong through the line. I am really happy with how he is progressing; he is right where you want him at this stage.'

A firm track — going that Prince Of Penzance had never relished — hindered his chances in the Group Two Herbert Power Stakes. He settled last from a wide draw and was never a threat, Michelle reporting that she was not happy with his action.

The stable form analyst Peter Ellis was far from despondent, noting that it was just too hard to run on from so far back and yet the horse had run his last 1000 metres in good time … 'That told me that he was on song.'

Prince Of Penzance pulled up well and was on track for a second Moonee Valley Cup. An ideal barrier (four), the softer Strathayr surface he had always liked. The blinkers were back on.

But he was racing against history, attempting to become only the second horse in seven decades to win the race twice, the first to win consecutive runnings since 1946.

For only the second time in his career Prince Of Penzance led. With 1200 metres to go another horse tried to tackle him, but he kicked up and kept rolling along. He straightened two lengths in front.

A lot can go through an owner's mind in a short time when a beloved horse looks like winning. They can picture the celebrations, taste the joy. Sam Brown could feel a much desired victory coming. This was the first time that all six of the Men In Hats Syndicate members had been together on race day and he so dearly wanted a big, gleeful joint celebration.

'I thought this was the moment,' he said, as he remembered edging closer to his brother so that they would be next to each other as Prince Of Penzance crossed the line. But he did not see the big flashy chestnut The United States beginning his run, a winning run.

Prince Of Penzance was defeated but not shamed. He had galloped so fast that his conqueror was able to smash the track record time held since August 2009. It was, as Sam noted 'one of his best runs even though he lost'.

'It was a sensational run, a magnificent ride,' Sam said.

'It is not often that you break a record and still get beaten,' Andrew Broadfoot added, while Mark Hall noted that he had finished in front of some big owners with the fourth-placed Bold Sniper raced by Her Majesty The Queen.

Michelle Payne was happy, telling John Richards that the run was better than the winner's — 'That is one horse we won't have to worry about at Flemington,' she said.

The initial disappointment of defeat soon wore off, and pride in the horse's achievement came to the fore. And then there was the realisation that by not winning he had avoided a weight penalty for his next start: the 2015 Emirates Melbourne Cup.

Chapter Seven

TOWARDS FLEMINGTON

THE final field for the Melbourne Cup is decided on the previous Saturday evening, after the running of the opening day of Australia's biggest racing week.

Owners, trainers, jockeys, media, officials and dignitaries converge on the VRC Committee Room from where the barrier draw — overseen by Chief Steward Terry Bailey — is televised.

Just three Victorian races — the Caulfield Cup, the W. S. Cox Plate and the Melbourne Cup — make a show of the barrier draw. For most races it is a computerised process that takes place behind closed doors.

But for the big races there is fanfare, especially for the Melbourne Cup.

Big displays of each horse's colours in the background. Terry Bailey onstage. Compere Jason Richardson enthusiastically announcing the results, interviewing the representatives of each competitor.

One at a time a horse's name is drawn out, someone involved with each runner invited to choose a miniature Melbourne Cup (a wonderful souvenir they get to keep) underneath which is a number … a barrier.

Groans as an owner draws a dreaded wide gate, smiles as another makes the ideal selection.

Usually the attention is centred on the favoured runners, the big-name trainers and jockeys. The barrier draw in 2015 was unique, with the most photographed participant being someone involved with one of the extreme outsiders of the field.

Stevie Payne.

As he approached the stage, Jason Richardson told onlookers, 'Steve told me he's after barrier one or two.'

There was no hesitation. So quickly did Stevie reach over and pick up a little Cup that his adored sister Michelle was still taking her place on the stage behind him.

'Yes!' Stevie cried.

'And he's picked barrier one!' Jason roared over the applause.

'He has the magic touch, your brother,' Jason said to Michelle.

Darren Weir agreed … 'A perfect barrier draw,' he said. 'I am really happy with that, it gives the horse a chance to get into a nice spot and a nice rhythm, it gives him the chance to run well. I'm not sure whether he's good enough but he's good enough to run top ten.'

Two days later the racing action headed to the CBD for the annual Melbourne Cup Parade, Swanston Street closed to traffic as thousands lined the street.

A horse drawn carriage led the way, Bart Cummings' son Anthony and grandson James proudly grasping his very first Melbourne Cup, won by Light Fingers in 1965. The great trainer was honoured by a procession of children donned in the silks of his twelve Cup winners, carrying the smaller versions of the Cup awarded to the winning trainer.

The 2015 Melbourne Cup, meanwhile, was held by VRC Chairman Michael Burn and Lord Mayor Robert Doyle. Both were beaming, so happy to be associated with the iconic trophy.

There was music, dancing, previous winners of the big race applauded … Efficient, Brew, Might And Power; all residents at Living Legends out near Melbourne Airport.

Held since 1983, this parade over the years has seen many a Melbourne Cup winner make a trip to town … the likes of Subzero,

Rogan Josh, Doriemus, Saintly, Arwon, Baghdad Note, Gala Supreme, Just A Dash, What A Nuisance, Piping Lane, Hyperno, Van Der Hum, Think Big and Black Knight admired by many.

Following the horses was a car for each runner, connections treated to a little glimpse of being a star. An Emirates red vest emblazoned with each horse's name was proudly worn, interviews were conducted.

It was a big thrill for a few of Prince Of Penzance's connections to be involved. Darren Lonsdale's daughter Emily remembers being starstruck sitting next to Michelle. Sandy McGregor was there too, sharing a special day with his son Charlie and daughter Jessica.

Channel 7 covered the parade, and its journalists spoke with Darren Weir and Michelle Payne.

'We're happy we've got him in the right order and we think the horse deserves his spot in the race,' Darren said.

'It is just a great thrill to be in our greatest race,' said Michelle. I am pretty confident we've got a good chance. It's just so exciting to be here — it's been a race that I've watched from when I was a kid. I used to get so excited; we'd stop at school every year and watch the race. To be a part of it is unreal.'

Michelle wouldn't just be part of the 2015 Melbourne Cup. She would be part of the race's entire history.

Chapter Eight

MELBOURNE CUP DAY 2015

3am Maddie Raymond stirs and rises from her warm bed. She has hardly slept. It is Melbourne Cup Day and she is one of those whose job it is to get Prince Of Penzance to Flemington.

4am Prince Of Penzance is unfazed as those around him prepare for the three-hour trip.

8am Bake Bakery in Adelaide serves its first bunch of themed cupcakes, horse faces staring up at hungry sweet tooths. 'They sold out really fast,' said head baker Jason McDonald. 'People love them, they are guaranteed to bring a smile to their faces.'

8.25am Eager racegoers stand patiently at Flemington's majestic gates awaiting the 8.30am opening time. Minutes later the first of 101,015 Cup Day enthusiasts charge through.

8.30am The first race day trains depart from Flinders Street and Southern Cross stations. At their peak they are running every six or seven minutes, and over the course of the day 308 trips transport over 48,000 racegoers. At about the same time a float leaves Warrnambool. Aboard is

Maddie Raymond and her co-workers Rachel Hernan, Jessica Dudley, Brittany Kirkman and Kellie Mitchell. As well as a security guard. And Prince Of Penzance.

8.35am Nobody at the Warrnambool stable wants to miss out on the big day so Jarrod McLean offers to drive a car full of staff to Flemington.

9am It is the era of the selfie, and as racegoers swarm into Flemington they take photos of themselves in front of every landmark … the finishing line, the statues of Melbourne Cup legends Phar Lap and Makybe Diva, of Bart Cummings and Roy Higgins.

10.30am Brunch is served in the birdcage marquees hosting celebrities and dignitaries. Sponsors lay it on; caviar and champagne, the wealthy and beautiful pose for photographers. The Cup Day's traditional yellow rose is worn by many.

10.40am The first of ten races is run and won, two-year-old Concealer winning the Group Three Emirates Airline Plate at debut. The Hong Kong based Zac Purton is aboard: 'It is always great to win a race on Cup Day. You know there are plenty of people watching, it's a rewarding feeling.'

11.20am The second race is won by Zarzali, whose jockey Glen Boss won three consecutive Melbourne Cups aboard the great mare Makybe Diva. The trainer is Bart Cummings' grandson James … Bart would've been proud.

11.48am The VRC's Melbourne Cup Tour Manager, Joe McGrath, poses with the Cup trophy as it makes its way to the mounting yard, where it is on display from noon.

11.59am Prince Of Penzance's part-owner Sam Brown, member of the Men In Hats Syndicate, does an interview from the track with 2GB radio — 'A bit of fun and banter.' He can tell the broadcaster doesn't really give his horse a chance.

12pm The J. B. Cummings AM Tribute Plate is the third race, won by De Little Engine, whose dam Arapaho Miss enjoyed Cup week success eight years previously, winning the VRC Oaks. Falamonte, Michelle Payne's first of two rides for the day, finishes fifteenth of the eighteen runners. She has plenty of time to put on her Cup colours, coincidentally the purple, white and green of the suffragette movement — they signify dignity, purity and hope. She shares the jockey room with the only other female jockey riding that day, Jackie Beriman. There is an overflow from the male room so there are also three overseas visitors: William Buick, Ryan Moore and Gerald Mosse.

12.40pm Race four is won by the promising four-year-old Malaguerra, whose seventh dam Rainbird won the 1945 Melbourne Cup.

1pm Connie Brown places a Prince Of Penzance scarf around the Bart Cummings statue. For a photo, for luck. Surely Bart would've been cheering for Michelle. He had, after all, provided her with her first Melbourne Cup ride, Allez Wonder, in 2009.

1.20pm Invincible Heart wins the fifth race, a 1000-metre dash down the straight. From Scone part-owner Warren Wruck cheers, to win a race on Melbourne Cup Day is to 'tick one off the bucket list'.

1.30pm Channel 7's Neil Kearney interviews Michelle Payne, asking if she is nervous. 'Not at all,' she says. 'I am excited to get out there and partner a horse I know really well.'

1.45pm A crowd of several thousand are congregating in the city with Melbourne Cup Day action beamed from Flemington to Fed TV, at 5000-square metres Australia's biggest fixed television screen. 'This has become quite a tradition in recent years,' says Matt Jones, Federation Square's General Manager of Program and Events. 'The day attracts an enthuiastic contingent of dedicated punters, many of whom dress up for the occasion, looking to experience the race in a novel atmosphere. We also have the advantage of being able to show off Cup Day to a wider audience of students and international tourists.'

1.55pm Members of the Men In Hats Syndicate congregate outside the owners' room at Flemington, plenty of happy snaps taken. Without consultation they have all turned up in the same coloured suits, but what really stands out is their Prince Of Penzance ties. 'Sam said if we didn't wear them we had to go home!' laughs Mike Botting.

2pm The Listed Lexus Hybrid Stakes is won in easy fashion by Don't Doubt Mamma. Her fourth dam, Denise's Joy, raced on this day in 1974, and a year later she won the VRC Oaks.

2.15pm The Melbourne Cup horses are saddled up. Form analyst Peter Ellis waits patiently, and as he heads to the mounting yard with Darren Weir they discuss tactics.

2.18pm Twenty-four horses primed for their biggest test stroll around the birdcage, their coats glistening. Some get a little on edge, but most take it in their stride — they are experienced stayers. Their trainers head to the mounting yard, including several who have won the big race before: Lee Freedman, David Hayes, Robert Hickmott and Gai Waterhouse. Gai's husband is proud of her achievement, noting that 'it is a very hard race to win; only two living New South Wales trainers have won it'. Les Bridge, back in 1987 with Kensei, is the other.

2.20pm Anthony and James Cummings, son and grandson of a Melbourne Cup legend, hand over the 2015 Melbourne Cup to VRC Chairman Michael Burn, whose wide smile suggests he is just about the proudest man on course.

2.25pm Twenty-four riders are presented to the crowd. They are born in eight different countries. Seven have already won the race, including Jim Cassidy. This is his last Melbourne Cup ride, with retirement beckoning. He takes off his Emirates hat and waves it to the crowd. For another, Damien Lane, this is a Cup debut. The rider of a roughie receives the most enthuiastic applause — Michelle Payne. Zac Purton rides the favourite Fame Game and is excited. 'No other race worldwide stops a nation like the Melbourne Cup does. It's always a special moment when you're a part of something like this.'

2.35pm One by one the Melbourne Cup horses enter the tunnel that leads to the mounting yard. The crowd's noise does not break the thick walls, the only sound is the clip clop of hooves.

2.36pm The horses emerge from under the ground, greeted by a sea of people. Every seat in the grandstand is taken, every viewing spot filled. Prince Of Penzance 'looks the best he has ever looked', notes owner Andrew Broadfoot.

2.45pm Darren Lonsdale presses record on his phone, taping Michelle Payne's final pre-race words. He leaves it on for the race.

2.46pm The horses canter to the barriers.

2.55pm They are at the gates. It is Paul Didham's fourteenth Melbourne Cup as official starter. He concentrates on the job at hand but admits to some pre-race nerves: 'It is a special day and it is a relief when you have them away without incident.'

2.58pm	Michelle Payne's father Paddy watches from his home in Ballarat, by himself with a cup of tea.
2.59pm	Michelle Payne aboard Prince Of Penzance thinks about her late mother Mary, her late sister Brigid and of Bart Cummings. In her book she later writes that she 'can feel they're up there watching over me. Prince has a few of us riding with him today.'
3pm	Tension, excitement, anticipation. The Melbourne Cup is about to be run. It's a big field but the horses load into the barriers without fuss. Despite this they run a couple of minutes late.
3.02pm	The barriers open, a flurry of colour. 'They're off,' says caller Greg Miles.

Chapter Nine

THE RACE

IT is the moment that comes as close to quiet as Flemington on Melbourne Cup Day can be.

The horses have entered the gates. All bets are on. Trainers have done everything they can. Owners tense up. Jockeys take a deep breath.

Ever so briefly there is a hush across the course. That tiny moment between the starter hitting the button and the barriers crashing open.

And then there is a mighty roar.

The roar cascades across the course. Those who have heard it before, who know it is coming, prepare to enjoy it.

Those at their first Melbourne Cup are overcome by it. There is no sound like it.

As the horses find their feet, as jockeys jostle for position, there is a gentler sound, that of punters talking out loud, figuring out where their fancy has settled.

At the jump Prince Of Penzance, who had been loaded into the gates first, who had been there the longest, dwelt ever so slightly.

He is a length behind the rest of the field. But a couple of backmarkers drawn out wider soon drop in behind him while there is room in front and around him.

Michelle Payne makes the most of that space, gently urging Prince Of Penzance forward. It is a balancing act; this is a horse who'd been known to over-race. Push too hard and he could react, do nothing and he would be too far back to be a winning chance.

For the first half or so of the straight Prince Of Penzance does get his head up. But he gives the impression not of a horse being silly or green, but of a horse who is such a keen competitor that he wants to get going. One who can't wait to show everyone what he can do.

It's a touch of arrogance.

At Flemington racegoers have wonderful access to the finishing line, as the public stands are right across from it. On Melbourne Cup Day there is not an empty spot.

When the horses pass the post for the first time the roar re-emerges. If it doesn't make your spine tingle you probably shouldn't be there.

Meanwhile on the track there is the thunder of hooves, the yelling of jockeys, the heavy breath of horses. As the field passes the stands Prince Of Penzance is tucked away, twelfth on the rails. It takes a keen eye to spot him among the colourful throng.

Around the back of the course, as Big Orange makes the pace, Prince Of Penzance is travelling well, his head on his chest as he trails Max Dynamite. The previous year's third placegetter, Who Shot Thebarman, is on his outside.

Approaching the 1000 metres there is a critical move. Michelle Payne gently slides Prince Of Penzance one off the fence. His owners watching can't quite believe how well he is travelling at this stage, though none of his rivals are yet feeling the pinch.

Nearing the turn his position is further improved — he is now three off the fence following Trip To Paris.

As the field fans into the straight they are eight across. Big Orange is still in the lead, Excess Knowledge on his outside, topweight Snow Sky next, then Trip To Paris.

Still behind them is Prince Of Penzance.

Straightening, there is another vital moment. Trip To Paris gives a little kick, then Sky Hunter on Prince Of Penzance's outside starts to tire.

This presents Michelle Payne and her horse with room to move. Had it been the other way around, had Trip To Paris tired, had Sky Hunter charged, Prince Of Penzance would've had nowhere to go.

But Michelle knew that Trip To Paris had the form to fight the race out. He was the right horse to follow.

There is 450 metres to go and Prince Of Penzance has clear air in front of him. Several others do as well, but they are not travelling like he is. He has the cheek, after 2800 metres, to be cruising.

He has eight in front of him, at the 300 metres seven.

He joins the leaders with 200 metres to go. He is flying. With 130 metres left he is in front. Max Dynamite, who had been close to him for most of the race, is making a gallant late run. The classy chestnut Criterion is digging deep.

Michelle is yelling as loud as she's ever yelled before. And there is a big smile on her face. Then she is at the line.

'History at Flemington!' cries race caller Greg Miles.

Chapter Ten

'HE JUST BURST CLEAR!'

USUALLY, 100–1 winners are greeted with polite muted applause. But this Melbourne Cup crowd was roaring. Punters jumping up and down, wild scenes erupting in the mounting yard from where the majority of owners were watching.

Darren Weir lifts Peter Ellis off the ground in a great big bear hug … 'I've won the Melbourne Cup!'

Oblivious to all of this is Prince Of Penzance, who runs boldly on as Michelle pats him on the right side of his neck, rubbing the left. A gentle moment, a private one between horse and rider even though it is shared by viewers in their millions.

Soon afterwards Sam Hyland, who is conducting horseback interviews aboard Bryan for Channel 7, catches up with Michelle … 'Michelle, this is something you dreamed of as a kid.'

Sam Hyland is the ideal person for the interview, a former jockey raised in a famous racing family. His father Pat won the 1985 Melbourne Cup on What A Nuisance.

'I was lying in bed last night imagining,' Michelle says to Sam, 'what if I am talking to you after the race?!'

And there she was, doing just that … 'unbelievable. A dream come true.'

Not for a second is Michelle lost for words. 'This horse is

awesome!' she declares, 'and Darren Weir, an unbelievable trainer to get him here like this today.'

Michelle says, 'All of his staff — Jarrod [McLean], Maddie [Raymond] and Tyson [Kermond] and all of them at Warrnambool, this is all to them because they got him here in the best shape he could be in, and I am just so grateful and thankful to them.

'When I won on this horse as a three-year-old here I thought, *This is a Melbourne Cup horse*. I felt like he would run the two miles out that strongly, but far out, I didn't think he'd be that strong!

'He was towing me into the straight and he just burst to the front; he was powering to the line.

'I had to give him a bit of a dig at the start, which I didn't want to do, to stir him up, but I had to, to hold my spot. We travelled quite strongly the whole way. He didn't really get to rest but he was still in a rhythm.

'From the 1000 metres everything just opened up. I got onto the back of Trip To Paris, who took me into the race. I was almost clipping his heels I was going that great, but I didn't want to check him. Then he just burst clear … it was unreal!'

Sam Hyland enjoyed every second of that interview. He was an apprentice at the same time as Michelle's brother Andrew and has stayed good mates with him, and has watched Michelle's career unfold.

Also a friend of Sandy McGregor, Sam has followed Prince Of Penzance since his first starts. As much as he could, he kept an eye on him during the race, watching from the 2000-metre mark as he waited for the winning jockey to get to him.

It was exciting and surprising, he says, for that jockey to have been Michelle. 'She was so relaxed and amazingly calm. It was a terrific moment in sport, a day I will never forget.'

Sam's fellow commentators were also delighted.

'They have come from all around the world to win this,' says Channel 7's Simon O'Donnell, 'and they couldn't beat the Kiwis!'

Fellow commentator Bruce McAvaney is clearly moved: 'What an incredible chapter has been written in the history of this great race.'

Staff from the Darren Weir stables converge on the mounting yard. Warrnambool foreman Jarrod McLean couldn't get in before or during the race, but nothing was stopping him being part of the celebrations.

As trainer of 2009 contestant Kibbutz (ninth to Shocking), he'd tasted Melbourne Cup fever previously and had thought that top ten finish to be a major thrill.

'But this is obviously much better!'

Meanwhile, Prince Of Penzance is welcomed by cheers as he approaches the grandstand. His neck is arched, the sign of a happy, proud horse. There is a spring in his step. He knows what he has done.

Stevie rushes to the track to lead Prince Of Penzance back. Down they come, past Flemington's famed roses, Stevie holding the lead rope aloft as Michelle throws her goggles to the crowd.

Maddie is behind, taking it all in. She joins in as the horse approaches the yard. Michelle leans down to give her a kiss. A couple of owners, Neil Laws and John Richards, are there too.

Journalists rush to Darren Weir, who smiles right through his interview with Channel 7's Peter Donegan.

'Darren Weir,' Peter says, 'you are part of Australian racing history.'

'An unbelievable feeling,' is the reply.

'You've gotta pinch yourself a bit,' Darren continues. 'What an absolute thrill and what an absolute credit to the team that I have at home.

'I kept saying to the owners that it is hard enough to get into the race, let alone win it. Just enjoy the day and hope like hell we can run top ten.

'I thought the horse was in great shape; there wouldn't have been many horses who'd had better preparations than him. He looked terrific in the yard, all the t's were crossed, the i's were dotted, we'd done everything possible, and we thought we had him here in great shape.'

There is a second interview with Michelle Payne, who tells Peter Donegan that 'my sister Margaret and I both had this strong feeling that I was going to win. I actually had a really strong feeling, but I thought, *Don't be stupid, it's the Melbourne Cup!* It was amazing, the lead up. I was so relaxed and I just couldn't work out why I was so calm. It was like it was meant to be, everything just fell into place.'

After describing a Melbourne Cup victory as 'everybody's dream' and thanking those who had stuck with her, Michelle then utters her most quoted words of the day: 'It's such a chauvinistic sport … I just want to say to everyone else you can get stuffed because they think that women are not strong enough, but we just beat the world.'

As she heads to the jockey's room for a brief respite Michelle passes Michael Moroney, who gives her a knowing smile. She is now a member of the elite club he joined in 2000 when Brew won the Melbourne Cup. It was, he says, a life-changer.

'When I won the 1997 VRC Derby with Second Coming nobody knew who I was,' he recalls, laughing at the memory of journalists around him looking for this Michael Moroney fellow. 'Three years later, when Brew won, everyone knew who I was!'

By this time Prince Of Penzance was making his way back to the stalls. He did not want to linger post-race; he had done his job. He was not taken by the fuss, much like his trainer!

Chapter Eleven

'BLAH, BLAH, BLAH'

THE presentation for the Melbourne Cup was already underway as Michelle, en-route pausing for handshakes and pecks on the cheek, made her way to the stage.

VRC Chairman Michael Burn spoke, as did Emirates' Barry Brown, representing the airline that has sponsored the big race for twelve years.

'Emirates is proud of its longstanding partnership of the Melbourne Cup carnival,' Barry said, adding that he was honoured to present trophies to Michelle and Stevie. 'It was incredible to be part of this significant moment in Australian history, one that I will never forget.'

The trophies were delivered one by one to owner Sandy McGregor, to Darren, to Michelle, to Stevie.

The speeches may well have been the most casual, most charming, most endearing in Melbourne Cup history. So often it is the case that after watching the big race those in television land switch off. But not on this day, Channel 7 reporting that ratings actually increased in the moments after the race.

People wanted to see this bit of history.

Handed the Melbourne Cup, Sandy McGregor held it high before passing it on to his excited daughter Jessica and taking the microphone.

'It's a dream to come here on Melbourne Cup Day and win it with a 100–1 pop.'

The sponsors, the VRC, the trainer, jockey, strapper and staff were all thanked and then: 'Fellow owners, today a dream became a reality — we have the Melbourne Cup.'

Darren Weir was next. 'Well, I don't really have a speech planned, but anyway I'll give it a bit of a go.'

'This is a dream for a Berriwillock boy,' Darren said, sending out a 'big cheerio' to his dad Roy and to his home town — 'I hope you got as much of a thrill out of this as I have.'

Once again all involved were paid tribute to, Darren noting that 'I have a lot of people I have to thank and there will be a lot of people I forget so I will apologise.'

To Michelle, who he was catching up with for the first time since the race, he said, 'You are an absolute credit to yourself, thank you for what you do for the stable and what you do for the industry.'

'I don't know what else to say,' Darren continued. 'There will be a party at Ballarat, a party at Berriwillock. See ya!'

Michelle Payne was next.

'I gave myself a little bit of time last night before I went to sleep to think if I won the Melbourne Cup what I would say. I thought to myself, *Don't be silly!* But it's nice to be able to dream and that is what racing is all about.

'I'd like to say it's a very male-dominated sport, and people think we are not strong enough and all the rest, but blah, blah, blah.'

This might've been the first time 'blah, blah, blah' has been incorporated into a Melbourne Cup acceptance speech!

'But you know what,' she continued, 'it is not all about strength; there is so much more involved. It's getting the horse into a rhythm, it's getting the horse to try for you, it's about patience.

'I am so glad to win the Melbourne Cup and hopefully it will help female jockeys from now on to get more of a go.'

The highest level of crowd applause was saved for the recipient of the Tommy Woodcock trophy, a miniature Melbourne Cup presented in remembrance of Australia's most famous strapper of all time, Phar Lap's best mate.

'Thank you very much, everyone at the stables,' Stevie Payne said. 'And thank you all the crowd we had today at the races. I hope you have a great night.'

As the presentations were taking place, Maddie Raymond was back at Stall 19 with Prince Of Penzance. She held a bucket to his mouth, scratched his nose. She stopped for hugs and kisses from friends, to receive well wishes from strangers.

At around the same time a colt by Potter out of Karen's Pick arrived a week late at Whittlesea. Breeder Jo Horton christened her Melbourne Cup Day foal 'Stevie'.

Meanwhile, Darren Weir was still talking to the press. 'It's a lifetime dream come true,' he told them. 'It is just the most unbelievable thing to happen to anyone.'

'Joint surgeries, a colic operation; what an amazing horse,' Darren enthused before thanking his 'magnificent staff'.

'I couldn't do it without them,' Darren said.

Asked about how he felt during the race, he said that he was happy while not wanting to get ahead of himself.

'I thought, *What a beautiful run the horse is getting*, but I remembered that last year I stood up and gave a couple of cheers when Signoff hit the front for about two strides, and I had to sit down again. I didn't want to go the early crow this time. At the furlong I was thinking, *Where's that bloody winning post?!*'

Sandy McGregor, part-owner of both Signoff and Prince Of Penzance, was watching Darren during that time. 'He was very animated over the final 150 metres, something you don't usually see from him.'

During the relatively short interview many people were acknowledged: 'I trained for Sandy's parents Stuart and Judith — good on you, they'll be watching from home.'

About Michelle: 'She's a great rider. She works hard behind the scenes, plenty of trips to Warrnambool, Terang, two hours there and two hours in the car back to ride one horse. It's great to reward her.'

And Stevie: 'He's a great kid to have around; the stable love him. You ask Stevie to do any job, doesn't matter if it's mucking out boxes, filling up water buckets or going to the races, the answer is always yes.'

The interviews continued and Darren didn't run out of words — 'Think of the most amazing thing that has ever happened to you,' he said to *The Australian*'s Chip Le Grand, 'and triple it.'

Asked if he was proud of repelling the international raiders, if he was pleased that the Cup remained in Australian hands, he laughed … 'I'm glad it's in my hands!'

Even the owner of the runner-up Max Dynamite, the multi-millionaire Rich Ricci, thought the local win a great one. 'It was better than us winning it,' he told the *Herald Sun*'s Leo Schlink. 'It's a fantastic story for racing.'

Chapter Twelve

'ONE OF THE BETTER PARTIES'

AT the on-course press conference Darren Weir was still in a talkative mood. 'I'd had four goals,' he told a packed room. A Swan Hill Cup, a Stawell Cup, a Ballarat Cup, a Melbourne Cup.

Where he was from, where he started training, where he trains now and, well, the last one is self-explanatory.

All achieved.

With the post-race festivities and presentations taking so long there was not much time for Prince Of Penzance's owners to make the most of the winner's room, though they managed to cram into a space too small for so many and make the most of the moment.

'The VRC's Michael Burn and Katherine Bourke were both so kind and generous to all of us,' said Andrew Broadfoot. 'They were excited and appreciated straight away just how good it was for the race to be won by a local horse with lots of owners and a female jockey.'

Fellow owner Mark Hall was happy to meet the ever-smiling Les Taggart, pourer of drinks in the owners' room. 'He is the most popular guy at the racetrack.'

Later, Mark had a chat with Denis Napthine in the committee room about colic, the politician who had trained to be a veterinarian amazed at the horse's comeback from such a setback.

While the owners, who headed up to the Flemington committee room to continue the celebrations as the last few races were run, were justifiably oblivious to all but their own joy, stewards were busy dissecting the Melbourne Cup.

It was unfortunately a race of considerable interference, with no less than eleven horses — Kingfisher, Sky Hunter, Criterion, Hokko Brave, Grand Marshal, Preferment, Gust Of Wind, Bondi Beach, Snow Sky, Who Shot Thebarman and Our Ivanhowe — striking trouble in the straight.

Some of them were under pressure at the time, others were travelling better. Though none were cruising to the extent that Prince Of Penzance was.

The stewards took a dim view of those to blame, visiting jockeys Frankie Dettori and Jamie Spencer charged with careless riding, the former suspended for a month and fined $20,000 and the latter suspended for twelve days.

Some two and a quarter hours after the Melbourne Cup, John Richards had to leave the committee room celebrations. He had another runner — Scarlet Billows in the Group Three Hong Kong Jockey Club Maybe Mahal Stakes. She raced away to an easy victory for the Darren Weir stable. What a day!

Leaving the track late, Andrew Wilson returned to the race day office to the lady who issued him his tickets, Glenys Buckley — he'd promised her a big kiss should his horse win the Melbourne Cup. He found that the staff had all gone home, but made good on his promise a couple of weeks later at Moonee Valley … 'she was very kind to us.'

Those involved in the Prince Of Penzance story were spread across the state and beyond, watching the action unfold from near and far, united by their delight.

Watching the race 'at the local', Dean Hawthorne proudly cheered home Prince Of Penzance. The horse had been at his Anzac

Lodge property at Cambridge for the year after he went through the sales ring; it was where he was educated and primed for his career as a racehorse.

'It was a big thrill,' Dean said, not only for himself but for the whole of the country. 'New Zealand breeders were doing cartwheels,' he laughed, admitting that he had a 'sentimental wager'.

'You did not have to have a big bet to do well at those odds!' Dean said.

In Queensland, owner Joe Dalton's wife Ros was not quite sure if Prince Of Penzance had won, but the roar in her lounge room let her know that he had. Her children were jumping and screaming, she was shaky and teary, her dog noticed that his people were distracted, making the most of the moment to eat the cheese off their plates.

Also up north, the TAB at the Reef Gateway Hotel, Cannonvale in The Whitsundays, ran out of money. It was the local for Joe Dalton, and his friends had been financially rewarded for supporting his horse.

Darren Weir's Financial Manager, Michael Leonard, watched from his lounge room, so moved that he cried, something in reflection that embarrasses him a little — 'My wife still brings it up whenever we have a dispute!' he joked months later.

The Cup had another positive for Michael, whose son's Brazilian girlfriend was in the process of applying for a Visa. When asked to produce proof of an appreciation for Australian culture she took a photo of herself with Prince Of Penzance and his Cup. 'I said to Darren I owed him one; he helped my future daughter-in-law stay in Australia!'

Darren's Account Manager, Luke Archibald, had a big day on course with mates and an even bigger night back at the stables — 'It was one of the better parties,' he said wryly. And Luke knows how to celebrate, he with a group of friends recently purchasing a second-hand mini-bus to ferry them to race meetings where they have a great time, win, lose or draw.

Racing Manager Jeremy Rogers, who had worked twice as hard as usual on a Monday to get things done in order to get to Flemington the next day, watched the race in the mounting yard.

He admits that he nearly didn't go: 'We had a fair bit on at work and I didn't expect a win.'

He is certainly glad he made the effort, being part of a great story, one that 'transcends the actual race'.

'If the second horse had won it would've been a matter of, *Yeah great, Frankie Dettori won*, and then we'd move on,' Jeremy said.

Instead, he said, it was a story of 'a horse unwanted at the sales who has overcome many surgeries and beat the world'.

On the day, Michelle's stellar ride was discussed at length. 'She rode the pants off twenty-three international jockeys,' joked owner Neil Laws, while Robbie Waterhouse talked of a ride of 'absolute perfection'.

Michelle's brother-in-law Kerrin McEvoy had his own Melbourne Cup ride, finishing seventh on Excess Knowledge. He didn't realise until pulling up what had happened.

'I was riding hard myself,' he told AAP's Mathew Toogood, 'and then I looked up and saw her in front and I couldn't believe it! It's an unbelievable thrill for the family.'

Hoofnote: The lucky ones who backed Prince Of Penzance didn't face long queues to collect from the bookmakers. He is only the fourth 100–1 winner of the Melbourne Cup, the others being The Pearl in 1871, Wotan in 1936 and Old Rowley in 1940. Though Robbie Waterhouse notes one astute punter had $3000 each-way at the big odds.

Chapter Thirteen

MELBOURNE CUP PERSPECTIVES

The Handicapper — Greg Carpenter

As the man responsible for allotting the weights to be carried by Melbourne Cup contenders, Racing Victoria's Chief Handicapper Greg Carpenter has a job of great responsibility.

Also Racing Victoria's Executive General Manager of Racing, he is one of those lucky men whose career is also a passion, Greg a true lover of the thoroughbred racehorse and one of the Melbourne Cup's biggest fans.

And he considers the 2015 Melbourne Cup to be one of the most memorable he has witnessed.

'In the book of Melbourne Cup history the Prince Of Penzance chapter will be the one most widely read,' he said.

It was a race that had it all.

Darren Weir, while already highly successful, still has 'the essence of a country trainer'.

Michelle Payne, who attained what 'every racing participant regardless of gender aspires to'.

An underrated, gallant horse who Greg describes as 'an outstanding staying talent'.

And best of all, Greg said, the mixture of people that are Prince Of Penzance's happy owners.

'The Melbourne Cup had been crying out to be won by a horse with grassroots ownership. And an Australian-trained horse at that,' he said. 'Prince Of Penzance showed everyone that the Melbourne Cup is still an achievable dream.'

Because of this, Greg said, 'Prince Of Penzance's victory was a very important one for Australian racing.'

And a win that came as no surprise to Greg, who had long held Prince Of Penzance in high regard.

'He came on to my radar in 2014 when he won the Moonee Valley Cup, and I thought then that he was the sort of horse who could be competitive in a future Melbourne Cup.'

Prince Of Penzance's gallant second in the Moonee Valley Cup a year later impressed Greg all the more.

'He led, setting up a track record breaking pace, and was only passed over the final fifty metres by a horse carrying less weight. His run was as good as, if not better, than the winner's.'

With his mind focused on his job, Greg does not take much notice of the punting side of racing, but admits to being surprised when he discovered that Prince Of Penzance had been such a big price.

Greg's Melbourne Cup Day is always a busy one and 2015 was no exception. He kicked that Tuesday off with media engagements, including ABC interviews with Red Symons and the Coodabeen Champions — 'That is always fun.'

Unable to secure his normal vantage position at Flemington on a walkway between the committee room and the owner's stand, Greg instead found a relatively quiet corner of the grandstand.

Here, someone else who had struggled to find a spot had placed himself: Darren Weir.

Occupied watching the race's historic finish, Greg didn't notice Darren's response, but he does recall hearing him let out a gasp once the field had settled.

Impressed by the dominance of Prince Of Penzance's winning

performance, Greg was also taken by his subsequent run in Adelaide, his tough first up second after racing wide in the R. A. Lee Stakes in late May.

'Having seen that run my view is that he is a horse who is consistently getting better as he races on. I am really keen to see what he does this spring as I think we are yet to see the best of him.'

The Starter — Paul Didham

The Didham name is a well-known one in Australasian racing circles.

Arthur Didham was a top-class jockey in New Zealand, later enjoying a successful career as a trainer, best remembered for his association with the popular stayer Igloo.

The winner of sixteen races in New Zealand and Australia, Igloo was second in all three of the Melbourne spring majors. In the Caulfield Cup he was gallant behind Gay Icarus, with Big Philou third and Gunsynd fourth.

A week later Tauto defeated him in the W. S. Cox Plate, and at his next start Silver Knight had his measure in the Melbourne Cup. Arthur's son Midge was aboard that day, and he went so close to a memorable double having won the previous year's Cup aboard Baghdad Note.

Midge trained for a couple of decades after his retirement from the saddle, and his sons Paul and John have both been jockeys, John lucky enough to have ridden in a couple of Melbourne Cups.

Midge's brother Mick also trained, and Mick's granddaughter Courtney Barnes is a successful apprentice jockey in New Zealand.

With the family name's link to Melbourne Cup history, it is apt that a Didham be an integral part of Melbourne Cup Day. And that job goes to Paul Didham, who since 2002 has been the great race's official starter.

'I was never lucky enough to get a ride in the Melbourne Cup so

I just had to get there in a different way,' he laughed.

Paul's first Melbourne Cup as starter was a memorable one. The tragic death of Jason Oliver leading up to his brother Damien's victory aboard Media Puzzle had ensured that it was a week of emotional turmoil for all who knew them.

'It was certainly a bizarre time,' Paul recalled.

The Melbourne Cup may be one of many races for the barrier staff, but they know it is special and they feel the 'heightened pressure'. As do the jockeys, Paul says.

'They are a lot less talkative before the Melbourne Cup, not as relaxed as usual. They are in the zone.'

While the race attracts a bigger than usual field, its contestants tend to be well behaved. These days many of them are world travellers, while the locals have been around many times before.

The 3200-metre start at Flemington is away from the crowd. The scene for the lucky few participating is quite a serene one, the noise of spectators merely background. The horses stay relaxed, even if their jockeys are not so much.

Paul knows, however, that the horses read their riders and those around them. 'It is a massive thing,' he said. 'If the jockey and the barrier staff stay calm, the horses will too.'

Paul considers every Melbourne Cup to be special, but the 2015 version was even more amazing than most. A 100–1 shot, the first female rider to win.

'It was a great day for Australian racing and the best racing story of the year,' he said.

Paul was just one year old when his father won the Melbourne Cup, but he can imagine how he felt when he crossed the line. He doesn't get to see the finish of the great race now, but he hears the roar.

And just like every lover of the thoroughbred, it gives him a thrill that no other race can quite match.

The Race Caller — Greg Miles

Greg Miles could not quite believe his eyes.

All was going well in this, his record-breaking thirty-fifth Melbourne Cup call. He is right on song as he brings to life the race listened to by millions.

Throughout the call he is accurate, descriptive, professional.

'Coming past the 300 metres, Excess Knowledge went to the lead narrowly. Here's Prince Of Penzance coming on down the outside.'

And then, a slight change to the timbre of his voice.

Surprise.

For the slightest moment Greg wonders if he has it wrong, could this really be … *I hope I've got the right horse*, he thinks.

'Prince Of Penzance for Michelle Payne, now Max Dynamite starts to charge home, Prince Of Penzance from Max Dynamite, Prince Of Penzance.'

What is going through Greg's mind at this stage?

'For those final few strides I was just thinking, *How good a story is this going to be?!*'

And then he finishes the call with four perfect words.

'It's history at Flemington.'

The 2015 Melbourne Cup so succinctly captured.

And yet totally unrehearsed. 'I didn't think I would be calling Prince Of Penzance as the winner,' he admits.

Not that Greg ever has set plans for what he will say in those thrilling final Melbourne Cup moments. He gets lost in the call, involved in the moment, and the right words just come.

'It is better not to have anything planned as it plays on the mind,' he says, not wanting to ever risk losing concentration.

For Makybe Diva's third Melbourne Cup he had a little something prepared, but she was one horse, he said, who made his job easy.

'A nation roars for a hero … a champion becomes a legend.'

Greg has a number of favourite Melbourne Cup moments. One was a defeat, the champion Kingston Town, oh so gallant behind Gurner's Lane.

And the history-changing Vintage Crop, the first northern hemisphere trained winner of the big race — 'The Irish horse will win the Melbourne Cup.'

And, of course, Bart Cummings' many great wins — 'Cummings going for ten and he's got it, Saintly wins it easily … Rogan Josh, Bart did it again.'

Or the champion chestnut Let's Elope — 'This magnificent mare dashes to the front.'

It's not often that the name of the jockey is mentioned in the final moments. In most races the caller doesn't even memorise the riders, as there's already enough to take in.

But then there are the special occasions, such as Media Puzzle in 2002 — 'Damien riding with the spirit of Jason.'

And in 2015 — 'Michelle Payne, Prince Of Penzance.'

Greg did not, at the time, realise just what a big price this winner was, though he knew that he was a long shot. It was, he says 'a big, big surprise.'

Not that there are any certainties in the Melbourne Cup.

'I never go into the race with preconceived ideas,' Greg says. 'I don't concentrate on the favourites. Every horse is equal.'

Until the end of the race, that is, when one horse stands alone.

Hoofnote: Greg Miles' 2014 Melbourne Cup call of the win by Protectionist was his thirty-fourth, equalling one of his heroes, Bill Collins. He called his first Melbourne Cup aged just twenty-two in 1981: Just A Dash. A couple of months after Prince Of Penzance's victory, Greg was awarded a Medal of the Order of Australia (OAM) for services to racing.

The Racegoer — Joan Walker

Attending every Melbourne Cup since the 1940s, Joan Walker is part of the race's rich history having bred and raced Reckless, who was second behind the Bart Cummings trained Gold And Black in 1977.

One of the most popular gallopers of his time, winning the Sydney, Adelaide and Brisbane Cups, Reckless was trained by Tommy Woodcock, who of course was best known for his association with the legendary Phar Lap.

Joan, who remembers the time when women were not allowed to cross certain lines at Flemington, has nevertheless never really regarded gender as a major issue.

In an interview with a Western Australian journalist when her horse was racing in the 1978 Perth Cup, Joan was asked what it was like to be a woman in racing.

'I didn't understand the question. I thought I was a person who loved racing, I just didn't see the need to differentiate.'

Four decades later and Joan feels the same way, enjoying the 2015 Melbourne Cup and admiring the feats of both the horse and rider, the gender of the latter immaterial.

'I felt the same way I always do after watching a great ride, that I had just witnessed the talents of an elite athlete.'

The Family — The Weirs

Darren Weir's family on course at Flemington on Melbourne Cup Day did not take a great deal of notice of the broadcast. It was, after all, drowned out in the noise of 101,015 enthusiastic and vocal racegoers.

They did, however, get their own version on the way to Ballarat that evening, Darren's thirteen-year-old nephew, Dayne Barry, giving his own rendition of the call.

A budding race caller whose calls at tracks like Mount Wycheproof and Burrumbeet can be heard on YouTube, Dayne (whose knowledge of racing statistics can rival any experienced professional) had a car full of his relations laughing … 'Prince Of Penzance has hit the lead and Nan is down!' he declared.

Nan being Darren Weir's mother Noelene, who was so overjoyed at the moment when she realised her son was going to win the Melbourne Cup that she more or less collapsed.

'My legs just went from under me,' the Weir family matriarch recalled, 'I remember thinking, *Oh my god, he is going to win the Cup!*'

What followed was somewhat of an exciting blur for Noelene, her daughter Melissa and her grandchildren, all of whom watched the big race from Flemington's historic old members grandstand.

Suddenly, a stranger was lifting them over a fence, then another was in search of security to let them into the mounting yard … into a frenzy of activity.

'There were people and cameras everywhere,' said Darren's daughter Bonnie. 'It was like paparazzi!'

Bonnie had been with her father en-route to Flemington, and recalls his pre-race anxiety being at a higher level than usual. 'He always chews his nails on the way to the races, but on that day he was doing it right up to the race.'

While Bonnie and her older sister Taige didn't watch the race with their dad, they soon caught up with him. There were hugs and happy tears aplenty.

And more still at the Weir Ballarat stables, which is where Darren's family headed.

For Bonnie the celebrations continued into Thursday, when she got to take a rather special gold trophy to school for show-and-tell.

'It was pretty exciting; we spent the whole day talking about the Melbourne Cup.'

Noelene, months later, admitted that she was 'still in disbelief', amazed that her son's 'dream had come true'.

'Right from when he first started training his ambition, like all trainers, was to win the Melbourne Cup.'

The Former Boss — Jack Coffey

When Prince Of Penzance crossed the Melbourne Cup finishing line, Jack Coffey, who had taken time off work to watch the day unfold from his lounge room, was as happy and emotional as can be.

'It was fantastic, unreal. The greatest, proudest time of my life,' said the man who was Darren Weir's first boss. 'My wife Sandra would've been so proud too. She loved Darren; she would've been so excited.'

Quickly onto the phone to a mate in Darren Weir's home town Berriwillock, Jack was keen to share the joy, not long after the race making his way to Ballarat to join in the stable celebrations.

'I reckon I was one of only two sober people there that night,' he joked. 'I had to work the next day!'

Darren Weir's journey from humble beginnings, from Berriwillock to Birchip to Flemington, is one that Jack has been delighted to follow — 'The triumphs of a young lad who had come from nowhere.'

Jack was born into a large racing family, one of ten children, many of whom are still involved. Austy is a trainer, and younger sister Briga Fliedner recently joined the Country Racing Victoria board.

Austy's son Harry has earned the respect of everyone in racing, fighting cystic fibrosis while forging his name as a jockey.

Meanwhile, Jack's sister-in-law Margaret is the mother of Luke Nolen, a talented rider whose name will always be linked with the great Black Caviar.

Jack travelled to the United Kingdom to witness that undefeated champion contest the Golden Jubilee Stakes at Royal Ascot in 2012, and has great memories of his nephew meeting the Queen.

Saturday 29 March was another proud day for Jack. The races were at Moonee Valley. Luke rode a winner, Harry rode his first metropolitan double, and Darren Weir had two as well. Harry was aboard one of those, May's Dream, daughter of the stable's Melbourne Cup runner-up She's Archie.

Lots of family ties. And more too, Darren providing Harry with his first provincial winner, his first city winner, his first country cup winner.

All great moments, but none bigger than the Melbourne Cup, a race Jack is thrilled to have some sort of connection with. And he's happier still to know Darren Weir.

'I cannot speak highly enough of him and I am proud to have played a small part in his life.'

The Home Town — Berriwillock

Cheers rang out in pockets across the tiny Mallee township of Berriwillock, birthplace of Darren Weir, on Melbourne Cup Day 2015.

The Golden Crown, Berriwillock's only business aside from the post office, which is open only in the mornings, was undergoing renovations and was not quite ready to open.

Its proprietor Bobby Borlase was hard at work on that Tuesday, a few mates dropping in to watch the races on a borrowed television, partaking in the great Cup Day tradition of a sweep.

At the Weir family farm, Darren's father Roy and sister Melissa sat comfortably in the lounge room. Darren's brother Chris was busy as usual, ducking into the house to watch.

There are only a couple of hundred residents of Berriwillock, and up until the horses entered the gates for the Cup it was as quiet as always.

Everyone was watching, most had a sentimental dollar or two each-way on a horse many had never seen, but who to them felt like a local.

Bobby Borlase's plans for the rejuvenation of the Golden Crown were in place, but they changed in a second, the moment when Prince Of Penzance drew clear to win the Melbourne Cup.

The moment when Berriwillock erupted, when Darren Weir's family looked at each other in disbelief, when every TAB within 100 kilometres realised they'd soon be out of cash.

'There was a mighty roar,' Bobby recalled, 'and I was tingling all over.'

Within minutes Berriwillock was loud. Locals wanting to share the excitement, driving up and down the streets, horns blasting, arms waving out of windows.

At Flemington, Darren Weir said, 'Cheerio to all the folk in Berri — this one's for you guys.'

And, 'Borlase better open that Berriwillock pub!'

The 'Welcome To Berriwillock' sign was added to, waving in the wind a banner: 'D. K. Weir 2015.'

'It was hectic, magnificent,' said Bobby, who remembers the look on Roy Weir's face as he joined in celebrations that night — 'He was over the moon; you couldn't wipe the smile off his face.'

Affectionately known as 'Boss', Roy — who passed away in April 2016 — was a man of few words, but as shown by an interview with the *Herald Sun*'s Matt Stewart, he was one with a wry sense of humour.

'Asked how he felt when Prince Of Penzance dashed clear at the 200 metres, Boss thought for a moment and said: "Well, if he'd tipped it to us maybe we'd have cheered it. But he never said anything."'

During the happy chaos that ensued on Cup Day, Bobby looked at the empty wall across from the Golden Crown bar and imagined what a great space it would be for a tribute.

And a week later it was there — wall-to-wall Prince Of

Penzance. The horse, Darren, Michelle, the Cup, the roaring crowd all in glorious colour. And now a tourist attraction in its own right.

'We've had people dropping in ever since to have a look at it,' said Bobby.

Including those who were lucky enough to be at Flemington on the day, such as local bus driver Julie who was delighted to find herself and her friends among the massive crowd.

'She played a bit of Where's Wally?' Bobby joked.

With the Golden Crown granted a temporary licence (and soon afterwards a full one) to help host a Melbourne Cup party, locals pitched in to help get the historic pub reopened in time.

And what a party it was. A week after the Melbourne Cup and Darren Weir was back, the population of Berriwillock keen to welcome him home and take their turn holding a Melbourne Cup.

Bobby will never forget his moment with the golden trophy — 'It was awesome!'

In March the party continued with the 'Back To Berriwillock' celebrations. A procession down the main street — shire horses, vintage cars, farm machinery, the local fire truck, a variety of floats from shearers to the Angling Club and 'Priscilla, Queen Of The Golden Crown'.

And of course Darren Weir, on horseback, the Cup held aloft, his daughters proudly at his side.

Berriwillock means a lot to Darren Weir, and Darren Weir to Berriwillock. Bobby Borlase said 'the win has given the place such a buzz', Darren's brother Chris adding that 'the race has put us on the map'.

The Vet — Dr Brian Anderson

While Dr Andrew Cust and Dr Ian Fulton (who had performed two of Prince Of Penzance's three bone chip operations) of the

Ballarat Veterinary Practice's Equine Clinic were at Flemington on Melbourne Cup Day, Dr Anderson was at work.

Though of course he was not going to miss the big race. The veterinary, nursing and reception staff gathered in the lunch room to watch. Prince Of Penzance, Dr Anderson recalled, seemed to 'come from nowhere'.

He felt admiration for Darren's training effort, for Michelle's ride. But most of all he thought, *How amazing is this horse?!*

'There is a school of thought,' he said, 'that once a horse has endured a colic operation that they are never quite as good, if any good at all.'

And so, not surprisingly, Prince Of Penzance is 'a great source of pride for everyone at the practice'.

Having been born, raised and trained in New Zealand, Dr Anderson has a natural affection for the Kiwi thoroughbred. He knows where Prince Of Penzance came from and who bred him, he knows the Pentire breed.

New Zealand, he says, breeds 'horses with big hearts and plenty of bone. And they can stay.'

And having been part of the team that saved Prince Of Penzance's life, he is more than a little bit fond of this bay gelding. Not that he was at first fully aware of just who his patient was. He knew his name, that he was a talent. It was not till later that his colleague Dr Andrew Cust, the Weir stable vet, told him that this was a Melbourne Cup prospect.

Who the horse is isn't the focus when he needs help. Dr Anderson's love of being a surgeon stems from his passion to fix things, and when a horse is sick that is the sole focus. There is time to think about who the horse and his connections are later on.

Dr Anderson loves horses. 'What a majestic sight is the in flight thoroughbred,' he says.

And he loves his job, even after a couple of decades still somewhat in awe of what he gets to do. 'To take a 550-kilogram animal, give it a needle, watch it go to sleep in a couple of minutes, perform a major operation and watch it wake up and recover … I still find this magical.'

He had originally planned to be a small animal veterinarian, but it was an uncle in New Zealand, also a vet, who pointed Dr Anderson towards horses, describing them as the most difficult and interesting of all animals.

And they don't come more interesting than Prince Of Penzance, whose Melbourne Cup victory is described by Dr Anderson as 'one of the crowning glories of my career'.

The Photographer — Peter Morganti

Peter Morganti has watched the amazing stories that are Prince Of Penzance, Darren Weir and Michelle Payne unfold through his lens.

A photographer by profession and passion, Peter has always considered himself lucky to work in a sport he loves, delighted when asked in 2010 to set up and run the Weir stable's Facebook page.

Happy with the 4000 or so followers of the page who would regularly log in to check on the Weir runners, Peter 'took great pleasure from watching it grow and grow from seconds after Prince Of Penzance crossed the line'.

And over the next few days, from 5000 to just under 12000.

One particular photo grabbed the attention of Facebook users — a casual snap taken by Peter of Stevie Payne before the running of the Melbourne Cup.

Almost not making it to the races, waking up feeling unwell, Peter at almost the last minute decided to get himself off his couch at Hamilton and make the trek to Flemington.

Having 'popped a couple of sudafeds', Peter made it to the track around an hour before the big race. As soon as he got out of the car he experienced the sensation of being in the right place at the right time … 'I was just so glad to be there.'

Nine days previously snapping photos for the stable at his home track, Peter had been talking to members of the Wilawl Go Racing Syndicate, whose Darren Weir trained horse Leica Day had been a winner on the day.

He knew how excited they all were about Prince Of Penzance's big assignment and promised he'd be there, concentrating on their horse. Those photos, he said, would be a good souvenir of the day they had a Melbourne Cup runner.

And so, despite feeling rather under the weather, Peter was at Flemington.

For the first forty-five minutes he hung around the stalls, and it was during that time he noticed Stevie leaning against the wall of the box next to Prince Of Penzance. It had already been a big day for him, but he had a moment to reflect. He had his arms crossed, he was staring with great concentration into the distance. It was as though he was visualising what was to come.

Peter picked up his camera and caught the moment.

After posting that photo on Facebook, adding the caption 'My life has changed from a normal bloke … to a Melbourne Cup winning strapper!' Peter was amazed by the response.

He was at the races, looking at his phone and watching the 'likes' and the shares fly in. Each time he refreshed the page, every couple of minutes, there'd be another thousand or so.

33,000 likes, 5704 shares, 605 comments.

'A truly great young man from a remarkable family.'

'A much deserved reward for an inspirational young man.'

'You have won the hearts of so many people Stevie … your love and passion for your job shines through.'

'I am so happy for this fella and his history-making sister … I shed a happy tear for them.'

'Hats off to you both and your family; you've touched so many lives.'

'My heart feels warm and fuzzy every time I see him … Daniel Craig, there's another man on my picture board.'

'In my fifty-five years I have never enjoyed watching a Melbourne Cup as much … all because of you Stevie and Michelle.'

'I'll say it over and over — disability does not mean inability!'

Michelle Payne loved the photo as well, since offering it to Down Syndrome Victoria who have plans to turn it into a keyring to sell as a fundraiser over the spring of 2016.

Peter was not sure where to photograph the Melbourne Cup from. His focus was on capturing the atmosphere, the people. He wanted to capture the pleasure on Stevie and Maddie's faces as they led Prince Of Penzance around the mounting yard, to be there when Michelle climbed on board.

It did not occur to him he was taking photos of the Melbourne Cup winner. He didn't even bother jostling for a place on the finishing line, instead taking his place forty metres past the post.

With the roar of the crowd behind him Peter could not make out Greg Miles' call of the race. His view of the big screen was not great, though he could make out that Michelle had her horse in a good position.

But he lost sight of Prince Of Penzance as the field approached the turn, as he was busy ensuring he had his camera ready for when they entered the straight.

Before he knew it Prince Of Penzance, the horse he was looking for but did not expect to see, was in front. It was like every other horse was in black and white, like the Weir runner was a blast of colour all by himself in front.

So surreal was the moment that at the 150-metre mark Peter put his camera down for a moment, frozen before the wonderful reality of what was happening in front of him — *You dickhead*, he thought, *take photos!*

He pulled the photographic trigger, for 100 metres before the line and another fifty after. And then he found himself a bit lost —

should he wait for the horse or head back to the mounting yard? 'I wanted to be in twenty places at once.'

Eventually deciding that the yard was the place to be, Peter came across Darren Weir's daughters Bonnie and Taige desperately trying to make their way to their father, blocked by the media throng.

'Grab my coat tails,' he told them, charging through. It was that moment, seeing the Weir family embrace, that really got to him, that sticks in his mind.

'I was wiping my eyes and taking photos at the same time.'

There was a hug so tight from Darren Weir that he felt his ribs were being broken but Peter wasn't feeling any pain, just elation to be so close to the action, to be in the thick of things with a group of people he'd come to know so well during the five years he'd been working as the stable's social media manager and photographer.

He had watched many a Melbourne Cup, thirty-five of them, from home. Here he was at the heart of it.

Back in his car Peter didn't budge for two hours. In his makeshift office he edited, downloaded and shared photos.

'History had been made and I owed it to Darren to get whatever I could out there, to showcase his wonderful achievement.'

From there it was on to the Ballarat stables, 'the first of many' drinks gladly accepted at around 8.30pm. He was still there when the *Sunrise* television crew arrived in the wee hours, at that stage heading to bed, i.e. his car.

'I drove home around midday, a bit worse for wear but feeling very happy, very privileged.'

Hoofnote: Prince Of Penzance owner Andrew Wilson calls Peter 'our eyes on the ground'. It is impossible, he says 'for us to be at every turn of our horse's career. Peter works tirelessly, travelling far and wide, his photographs capturing the moments we miss.'

The Strapper — Stevie Payne

'Don't get beat, I've got my money on you,' said Stevie Payne to his sister as Prince Of Penzance headed out onto the track.

He'd had his $10 each-way on, and while many having a punt had done so for sentimental reasons, for Stevie it was a matter of confidence.

'He will go close,' he'd been telling all who'd asked about Prince Of Penzance's chances.

Spending the day loyally at the horse's stall, Stevie was excited but still composed, his calm aura no doubt rubbing off on Prince Of Penzance.

'Prince Of Penzance can get a bit flighty pre-race,' said owner Sam Brown, 'but with Stevie on Cup Day he was so relaxed, I couldn't believe it.'

As the horses entered the mounting yard, Stevie was deep in concentration, holding onto one side of the horse, with Maddie Raymond on the other. He was not too serious, though — as photographers zoomed in he smiled and waved.

Watching from the mounting yard, Stevie had two reasons to cheer: for the horse, for Michelle.

As is the case when things that seem too good to be true actually do eventuate, Stevie was in shock when Prince Of Penzance crossed the line, grabbing onto Maddie and refusing to let go.

Channel 7's Neil Kearney grabbed a quick interview — 'Stevie Payne, you're the man of the moment.'

'A great moment, a great win, a great ride, ten out of ten,' Stevie enthused, thumbs up to the camera.

Not needing much coaxing to head out to the famous rose-lined path to grab the horse's reins, Stevie was beaming. Photographs of those moments provided some of the day's most endearing images.

Instant celebrity status was endowed upon Stevie, his hand grabbed in celebration by racegoers leaning over the fence, keen to give him a high five and have a selfie taken with him.

Michelle dismounted from the horse into Stevie's arms. It was a tight embrace.

While not Prince Of Penzance's usual strapper, Stevie was part of the Melbourne Cup action from the previous weekend. So many enjoyed that historic moment where he drew just the right gate at the barrier draw.

'Stevie won us the Melbourne Cup,' Sandy McGregor would go on to say, still ruing the much trickier gate fifteen his fourth-placed Signoff had drawn in 2014. 'I should have got Stevie to draw it last year!'

'I remember watching the barrier draw in the nursery car park on a phone,' Sam Brown recalled. 'Stevie waltzed up and went bang, picking barrier one. I had tingles down my spine and a tear in my eye. That was truly a special moment, one at the time I did not think could get topped!'

It was the wish of the stable and Prince Of Penzance's owners that Stevie be involved on Cup Day, this texting session between Darren Lonsdale's daughter Emily and Michelle Payne taking place on 27 October, a week before the big day.

> Emily: could we make a special request and have two strappers on Melbourne Cup Day … we want to add Stevie to our team because he always seems to have the luck.
>
> Michelle: haha I was already thinking that actually. I'll ask Darren and see what he says.
>
> Michelle: spoke to Darren, he said that would be okay. Sandy had one request that Stevie picks the barrier.
>
> Emily: haha. He might pick the perfect barrier for us.

'I was rapt when I heard that Stevie was strapping the horse with Maddie,' said Sam Brown. 'I know he is a good luck charm around the stable. He has strapped a few Group One winners and the horses love him.

'All the owners admire Stevie. He is always smiling and just speaks what he thinks. What a legend.'

Stevie began working at the Darren Weir stables, on the request of his father Paddy, around a decade ago. His boss is by no means an easy marker but he has plenty of respect for hardworking employees, of which Stevie is one.

'No job is too big or small for him,' he said. 'Whether it is cleaning out a stall or fetching hay he is happy to do it. He never misses a day. He is happy around horses and they respond to him. He's a little beauty.'

'Stevie has been working with Darren for as long as we have been with the stable,' said Prince Of Penzance owner Andrew Wilson. 'He is extremely hardworking, and whatever job he is given to do he just does it without questions or complaints. He is great with the owners, has a unique sense of humour and has embraced his celebrity status since the Cup.'

In an interview with AAP the day after the Melbourne Cup, the Down Syndrome Association's Tracylee Arestides admitted to being excited.

'It is so nice to see a person with Down syndrome being presented as a regular guy who is good at his job,' Tracylee said. 'Stevie is special because he is a really good strapper and he has been doing it for ten years. It's not having the Down syndrome that makes him special.'

Enjoying the limelight at the Cup Night parties, Stevie made the most of every moment. 'The best part,' he cheekily said, 'was getting photos with the girls and the free beers at the pub.'

Chapter Fourteen

THE EMERALD HOTEL

IT was not a normal Tuesday afternoon at The Emerald Hotel, South Melbourne.

Since around 10.30am it was busy, Melburnians revelling in their annual day off for a horse race. Functions had been booked out for months, the bar was packed, punters were keen to take part in every sweep offered.

There ended up being about thirty of those; every time someone declared that they had missed out another was started. Everyone wanted a horse, a piece of the action. Pieces of paper declaring who had drawn which horse were pinned to the walls.

Walls which are decorated with racing memorabilia — a framed photo of the W. S. Cox Plate winner Dane Ripper, along with jodhpurs signed by jockey Damien Oliver.

A set of the mighty Super Impose's silks, a photo of Phar Lap after his historic victory in the Agua Caliente Handicap in Mexico in 1932.

This is a racing pub.

Faye Lewis, who has run The Emerald with her family for the past twenty-five years, loves the Melbourne Cup. She tries to get to Flemington for the big day but in 2015 there was just too much on.

At 4.30pm, when the phone rang, it was still busy. Those dressed up in race day finery in the dining room had begun to weary, but those celebrating wins and lamenting losses were still going strong in the bar.

At the other end of the phone was Sandy McGregor, a regular at The Emerald for a couple of decades. Could he bring the Melbourne Cup party to South Melbourne?

A flurry of activity ensued, the dining room cleared, furniture shifted, sausage rolls removed from the freezer. There would be children, so someone quickly nicked up to the local supermarket for lolly supplies.

Faye Lewis has often been asked since if this was a planned party, but how, she asks, could anyone have foreseen such a thing?

The Emerald was still busy when the Prince Of Penzance party began to arrive a couple of hours later. The celebrations had spilled out onto the street and so when Darren Weir arrived, holding the Cup aloft, he was greeted with a roar both outside and in.

'Berriwillock Culgoa!' he cried … his home town, Faye's home town. Just fourteen kilometres apart in the Mallee where, Faye says, 'everyone knows everyone else'.

Faye and her husband ran the Kaneira Hotel at Culgoa, her parents and grandparents before them. For forty-seven years it remained in the family.

So apt then that the celebration of a Mallee Melbourne Cup victory be held at The Emerald. And what a night it was.

Upon hearing of the party, media began to arrive, Stevie Payne taking control. Channel 7 interviewed Darren Weir, who could not wipe the smile off his face.

'It has been unbelievable,' he told them. 'I haven't had much of a chance to answer my phone, but I had a look before and there are 360 messages. That gives you some idea of the support we've been given.'

Michelle Payne kept a clear head, telling reporters that she didn't have much to drink … 'I didn't want to get drunk and not remember the night!'

Arthur Rickard had no such reservations, admitting that by the end of the night, when his daughters Jenny and Sue were battling to get him into a taxi, he was not making much sense. 'I was speaking in Braille,' he laughed.

Sam Brown remembers arriving at the hotel, greeted by a sea of lights from TV station cameras. The atmosphere, he said 'was like winning a footy premiership but better.'

The Cup was passed around, beer drunk out of it, many a photo taken. Sam was amazed by the look on people's faces as they held it, shaking his head when the realisation hit him … 'Holy shit, we won the Cup, that's ours!'

With so many people around, Sam wondered at times if he'd ever see the Cup again, joking with Darren Lonsdale, 'Mate, we might be the first Melbourne Cup owners in history to lose the trophy!'

'We decided to stand by the door for a bit and do our own security,' Sam laughed.

'It was a great venue,' Andrew Broadfoot said, amused at seeing Darren Weir behind the bar pouring beers.

ABC television turned up to interview connections, but the task of keeping the room full of revellers quiet for long enough proved impossible.

Nick Williams, son of Lloyd Williams who has four Melbourne Cups of his own, dropped in just to congratulate the owners and share a drink.

Jarrod McLean from the Warrnambool stables was there too, part of a big day that began at the beach. He is full of admiration for Prince Of Penzance. 'He is such a competitor,' he said. 'He has been through a lot but has come through the other side on top. His setbacks have made him stronger.'

Among the last to leave just before 3am were the Wilson and Laws families. It had been such a fun night, one they did not want to end, all the more enjoyable for it having been unplanned and informal. It was not the usual big race celebratory dining for Prince

Of Penzance fans, rather platters of sausage rolls and snake lollies. 'We loved that!' Andrew Wilson said.

When Darren left, on his way to another party at his Ballarat stables, The Emerald party was still raging.

'It was just a fabulous night,' said Faye Lewis, 'something that will never happen again.'

Around 350 people turned up, many needing help hailing taxis in the wee hours.

The next day a row of empty beer kegs stretched down Clarendon Street. Plans were being hatched to commemorate the day with a collage of photos for the bar wall.

It was a great thing for Faye to be involved in a Melbourne Cup celebration.

As is the case with so many Australians, the race is part of family folklore, with her father loving to tell the story of the day he and a group of friends headed to Flemington to back Old Rowley because someone knew his jockey Andy Knox. They had a great day, stopping on the way home just out of Bendigo to celebrate at a country dance.

Successful in the 1940 running, Old Rowley was the last 100–1 winner of the Melbourne Cup.

As The Emerald party continued on into Wednesday, others were underway, such as that at a nightclub at the nearby casino.

Sam Brown and fellow members of the Men In Hats Syndicate arrived at 1.30am. They'd rung ahead but they were at first refused entry … until it was realised who they were, what they'd done.

'The Melbourne Cup opens doors!' he said.

Right into the swing of things on the dance floor, Sam was amazed to look across the room at one stage to see the Melbourne Cup being passed around. It was following him.

'I tried to get my hands on it again but people weren't prepared to part with it!'

There were other Melbourne Cup participants relaxing after their big day. When Sam discovered that super star jockey Frankie

Dettori was one of them he told the club manager that he just had to meet him.

Frankie obliged with a photo but didn't seem to be in the best of moods. He had, after all, flown across the world for his fourteenth crack at the Melbourne Cup, for the second time finishing runner-up and copping a fine and suspension.

'We didn't let him know who we were, we thought it best not to rub his nose in it!'

Meanwhile Darren Weir's staff were celebrating at the Ballarat stables. Their master arrived late, his first words: 'I wish you could all feel like I feel now!'

'It was a brilliant moment,' said the stable's social media manager and photographer, Peter Morganti. 'It was like a King returning to his palace. So much respect for the boss, lots of yelling and clapping, many tears.'

Those present may not have known exactly what a Melbourne Cup winning trainer felt like, but they were nevertheless just as euphoric.

At the time working as the stable's owner services manager, Katrina Wood has great memories of the night, one that saw family, friends, staff, vets, farriers, locals and owners converging on Darren's famous entertainment room.

'The race was played on the big screen over and over,' she recalled, 'and Prince Of Penzance was cheered home with the same amount of feeling and gusto every time!'

The music pumped, the drinks flowed. It was, Katrina said, 'an epic party'.

Darren's daughter Bonnie had the night of her life. 'It was great,' she enthused, remembering that 'we had to order over a hundred pizzas to feed everyone!'

Maddie Raymond, who'd been up since 3am driving from Warrnambool to Flemington and back, and then to Ballarat, arrived at around 11pm, wearing the most perfect of outfits — the Melbourne Cup rug.

'I didn't think I'd last, but when I got to Ballarat I was ready to party! Everyone was in such a good mood and the party carried on right through the night. So many speeches were made and stories told about how people dream of winning the Cup. I got to bed at about 4am and woke up with a very sore head, but I don't think what had actually happened had sunk in yet.'

Jarrod McLean, foreman at the Warrnambool stables, also made it to Ballarat (via The Emerald). Knowing, however, that he had the usual work day following (proud that every horse was worked as planned … 'we didn't miss a beat') he was careful not to drink too much.

But he made it through to 4am, laughing that 'it's the first time I've been up past midnight since I was twenty-one!'

While the Warrnambool staff headed to bed, the party was still bubbling along as television stations began to arrive. At 7am Darren, still in his race day suit minus tie, was interviewed along with Michelle Payne's father Paddy by Channel 7's *Sunrise*.

It was an interview interrupted by a streaker showing off his wares in the background!

Still the celebrations continued, Katrina admitting defeat at 9.30am, Darren deciding to skip Kyneton Cup Day … 'We might kick on a bit here, keep the party rolling.'

And roll on it did, right through to Ballarat two days later.

Chapter Fifteen

BALLARAT'S MELBOURNE CUP

'IT'S OUR CUP' exclaimed Ballarat's local newspaper, the *Courier*, the day after the Melbourne Cup.

Adorning the front page was a picture of Michelle Payne, returning to scale past the famous Flemington roses, leaning down from Prince Of Penzance to affectionately pat her brother Stevie on the head.

This is a proud city, one that has claimed Prince Of Penzance as its own.

And they are entitled to. Darren Weir trains there, Michelle Payne was born and raised at nearby Miners Rest and on 10 February 2001 she made her riding debut at Ballarat race course, winning aboard the Paddy Payne trained Reigning.

The cheers that rang out for Prince Of Penzance as he won the Melbourne Cup were louder at Ballarat than anywhere. It did not take long for the City Of Ballarat to announce that a celebration would be held in honour of the historic victory.

And so the rural city's 98,000 or so inhabitants were summoned.

'Sturt Street will be closed for three hours for a party which will celebrate the city's newest heroes Michelle Payne, Stevie Payne and Darren Weir … and everyone is invited.'

Friday 6 November dawned overcast and drizzly in Ballarat,

but that was not going to deter anyone. Locals turned up in their thousands … school children holding up drawings of the horse, toddlers dressed up in Prince Of Penzance's silks, fans handing flowers to Michelle.

And one particularly proud Ballarat resident, Prince Of Penzance part-owner John Richards, who could not help but be impressed.

'The council did a terrific job,' he said, 'there was a lot of fanfare, all organised very quickly, almost spontaneously.'

A stage was set up outside the Ballarat Town Hall, Mayor John Philips presenting Darren, Michelle and Stevie with gold-plated mining pans as he noted that, 'Gold put Ballarat on the world stage … and now it has happened again.'

While the ovation for trainer, jockey and of course Stevie was resounding, the Mayor was greeted by only muted applause … 'I am going to have to buy a horse,' he joked, 'if you want popularity, you need a horse.'

Michelle Payne was almost overcome by her home town's response as she made her way onto the stage. 'Fantastic isn't it?' she said to Channel 7's Neil Kearney. 'It doesn't get more special than this, it's an overwhelming atmosphere.'

'I'd like to say a huge thanks to everybody for coming today,' she said to the crowd. 'I'm a proud Ballarat girl and to come up here and see all you guys is unbelievable. I'm so proud to be here and to have won a Melbourne Cup.'

Darren Weir was also amazed. 'I was happy to get involved. I thought a few people might turn up, but geez, when we got there the people that were there and the reception they gave the horse and Michelle and Stevie and also myself … it was an unbelievable feeling.'

Ballarat Turf Club CEO Lachlan McKenzie was also there, describing the Cup win as 'the best day in Ballarat racing history, without question'.

Darren Lonsdale thought it a great opportunity to spend some quiet time with his horse, sneaking away during the presentations for a pat.

Several other of Prince Of Penzance's owners were in attendance, Greg Williams proudly noticing that the horse stood stock still, watching himself as the replay of the Cup was shown on a big screen.

Andrew Wilson remembers that also. And he too was staggered by the turnout. 'The crowd just built and built,' he said.

'It was packed,' added Pam Wilson. 'They closed the main street but the horse didn't care; he took it all in his stride.'

He was quiet and calm as he was paraded around and around the Queen Victoria monument, while Stevie held the Melbourne Cup as high as he could.

Big race winners are usually resting at home after their moment in the sun. Not Prince Of Penzance.

Two days after the Cup he was at his local racetrack, Maddie Raymond leading him around the Warrnambool mounting yard during their Oaks Day meeting. Stevie was there too, still wearing his strapper's bib, again proudly grasping that gold trophy.

Also a special guest at Warrnambool's Civic Green, Prince Of Penzance was once again admired and applauded, local racing fan Melissa Boswell-Happ excited by the chance to have her daughter Jess photographed with a Melbourne Cup winner.

'It was amazing to have him there not even three full days after the Cup,' she said. 'It just goes to show what sort of temperament he has; he was a pure gentleman.'

Jarrod McLean is amazed how well behaved Prince Of Penzance is at each of his engagements, recalling the first time he saw him at Warrnambool.

'As a young horse he was a bit of a handful. He has a beautiful temperament but he has always been really alert and quite headstrong. The sort of horse who if he wants to go somewhere will just walk over the top of you.'

But while being admired by fans, Prince Of Penzance was on his best behaviour, as if he knew of his own importance.

'He was just happy to take it all in,' McLean said.

The following Wednesday, Prince Of Penzance headed to Berriwillock, the Buloke Shire Council holding a civic reception at Darren Weir's home town. They blocked off the main street, put on a barbeque and people came from everywhere.

Country Racing Victoria provided a big screen with all the Melbourne Cup Day action replayed.

School kids held a 'Congratulations Weiry' banner before bombarding the trainer with questions about Prince Of Penzance: Where does he live? What does he eat?

Adults also got into the spirit of things, brandishing Darren Weir masks, before sharing a drink with him at the Golden Crown. The pub's Bobby Borlase had to source beer from three nearby towns to cope with demand.

More speeches for Darren. 'I used to dream about this,' he said. 'And what I say to you kids is that it's good to have dreams. If you work hard, sometimes they come true.'

Everyone wanted their time with Darren. The party went well into the wee hours, Bobby Borlase recalling that 'the band was still blasting at 4am'.

Ten days on and it was Ballarat Cup Day. There were 12,000 on course to witness the Chris Waller trained Junoob win the feature race, but most of the attention was on Prince Of Penzance in his glorious Melbourne Cup rug.

And again, Darren, Michelle and Stevie were posing for photos, shaking hands.

Part Two

THE BEGINNINGS

'A nice, straightforward horse.'

Chapter Sixteen

A CUP STAR IS BORN

IN recent times there have been around 12,000 to 16,000 foals born in Australia each year. Just a handful of them will make it to the Melbourne Cup, where they will be taken on by horses from New Zealand, Europe, Japan, England, Ireland and occasionally the United States.

Between them, those countries produce around 50,000 foals a year.

In a Melbourne Cup there will be horses aged from four to seven, sometimes a little younger or a little older. In the average running four foal crops will be represented.

That's a pool of approximately 260,000 horses.

Each year just one of those will win the Melbourne Cup.

◆ ◆ ◆

It is 20 November 2009. A baldy faced bay colt arrives in the world. Like any thoroughbred he is the culmination of generations of careful breeding, of patience, study and thought.

So many people contribute to the existence of each horse. His story is one of many threads.

Bred by Jungle Pocket Pty Ltd and Rich Hill Thoroughbreds,

Prince Of Penzance is a son of Pentire and Royal Successor, both of whom have their own stories.

A grandson of the legendary Northern Dancer, Pentire was bred by Lord Halifax who had, with his father Charles Wood the 2nd Earl of Halifax, bred and raced the 1978 Epsom and Irish Derby winner Shirley Heights.

While Shirley Heights was at his dam Hardiemma's side she was in foal to another winner of the Epsom Derby in Blakeney, the foal inside her being Bempton, who would go on to be the grandam of Pentire.

Bempton produced Pentire's dam Gull Nook by a mating with one of the true greats of the turf, Mill Reef.

The American bred, English trained Mill Reef won twelve of his fourteen starts, including the Epsom Derby and the world's most prestigious weight-for-age contest, the Prix de l'Arc de Triomphe.

In August 1972, in preparation for a second attempt at that race, the four-year-old Mill Reef stumbled as he worked. That's all it was, a stumble, but one with catastrophic repercussions.

The sesamoid bone was the first to break. As Mill Reef gallantly took his next step the pressure of his weight crumpled the rim of the pastern, and two-and-a-half inches of bone broke off the cannon (shin bone).

His rider John Hallum, having 'heard a terrible crack', dismounted within seconds, a dismayed Ian Balding rushing to his side.

In his memoir *Making The Running*, the trainer remembers Mill Reef's astonishing calmness. 'He was remarkably relaxed, picking grass and not even sweating.'

A float was quickly summoned, though nobody knew how they would get the severely injured horse into it. But they were dealing with a special horse.

'In one of the bravest and most intelligent reactions I have ever seen from a racehorse,' Balding wrote, 'Mill Reef jumped virtually unaided half way up the ramp and with our assistance somehow scrambled the rest of the way.'

Unwilling to risk transporting his champion any further, Balding arranged for the operation to take place at the stables, a temporary hospital set up in the apprentice jockeys' gym.

With his joint feeling 'like a bag of marbles', it was never going to be an easy operation. For seven hours Mill Reef was under the surgeon's knife, the fragmented pieces of bone secured with screws and a plate.

Years later, Prince Of Penzance's surgeon Dr Brian Anderson would observe that the great horses are those most likely to emerge from operations well, and Mill Reef was such a horse.

'He was as usual sensible,' Balding wrote, 'and with a little help from us got up at the first attempt with the minimum of fuss.'

Retired to The National Stud at Newmarket, Mill Reef made his mark as a stallion, siring sixty-two stakes winners. One of those was Gull Nook. She raced just four times, but was able to defeat fellow Mill Reef filly Mill On The Floss in the Group Three Ribblesdale Stakes at Royal Ascot.

At stud she would fare well, producing eight winners, the best of whom was Pentire. He was a horse with more of the look of his dam's sire Mill Reef than of his own sire Be My Guest.

Be My Guest undoubtedly contributed to the Pentire success story, however. Sold for a then record-breaking price as a yearling, he was a good racehorse without being a star. But at stud he excelled, siring sixty-six stakes winners and helping to put Coolmore Stud on the map.

While not a particuarly big horse, Pentire could gallop with one of his fans, bloodstock agent John Foote noting that 'he had a phenomenal turn of foot … he was one of those small horses who can pick up and go through the gears quickly.'

It is a turn of foot seen in the best of Pentire's progeny, that shown by Prince Of Penzance at the end of the 3200 metres. He was flying as others were tiring.

It was Pentire's mating with the American bred Royal Successor that produced his Melbourne Cup winning son. She had not made it to the races and she had failed to fire during her initial years at stud in Japan.

But lying dormant in her genes was talent. Her sire was the great Mr Prospector. Born the same year as the legendary Secretariat, he won seven of his fourteen starts but never aspired to championship status on the track.

But he did at stud. The sire of 177 stakes winners, he left an enduring mark on the thoroughbred internationally. Prince Of Penzance is the fifth Melbourne Cup winner, after Ethereal, Media Puzzle, Efficient and Shocking, to have Mr Prospector in the bloodlines.

Royal Successor was born in 1999, the same year that her sire died in his stall at Claiborne Farm, Kentucky, from complications of a colic attack.

Claiborne Farm has been home to many a famous thoroughbred. Nasrullah, Round Table, Sir Ivor, Secretariat, Danzig and Nijinsky II are buried there.

Countless others of influence have been bred there, such as Robert Sangster's French Derby winner Caerleon, a son of Nijinsky II. A highly successful stallion, he was represented by 120 stakes winners, one of whom was the filly Only Royale.

A tough, classy and consistent mare, Only Royale won her first four races from May to September 1992. She would progress through the grades to become the first two times winner of the Group One Yorkshire Oaks, a historic race first contested in 1849.

She also ran in two editions of the Prix de l'Arc de Triomphe, unlucky both times. In 1993 she finished a gallant fifth after striking severe interference just 300 metres from home, and a year later a close up seventh having been held up for runs.

Only Royale was bred at Barronstown Stud, Ireland. Established in 1980 by David and Diane Nagle, it has been home to twenty-five Group One winners, one of whom provided his breeders with a proud moment contesting the 2006 Melbourne Cup.

The great race was won that year by the Japanese raider Delta Blues, bred by Northern Farm who, under the banner of Jungle Pocket, are the co-breeders with Rich Hill of Prince Of Penzance.

The Barronstown runner was the splendid galloper Yeats who from 2006 to 2009 won four runnings of the Ascot Gold Cup, his achievement recognised with a statue in the Royal Ascot parade ring. Third favourite as topweight in the Melbourne Cup, he did not have the best of runs but was far from disgraced, finishing seventh.

'The Melbourne Cup gets plenty of publicity in Ireland,' said David Nagle. 'We always watch it and were thrilled to have a runner and happy to finish seventh. We didn't realise that Prince Of Penzance was Only Royale's grandson, but we are obviously delighted!'

David remembers Only Royale as a nice type of filly, easy to manage, with a good temperament. He still has her foaling report from Coolmore Stud on record … 'easy foaling, a good foal'.

A photo of Only Royale shows her staring straight at the camera, bold and confident.

Her dam, the Group Three winner Etoile de Paris, is also fondly remembered by the Nagles, David describing her as 'a lovely quality mare and a good racehorse'.

While Only Royale was Etoile de Paris's most successful runner, she is also ancestress of a number of other classy horses, including the South Australian Group Three winner Torezal.

Etoile de Paris's dam Place D'Etoile was also talented, a Group Two winner who produced seven winners, including the Irish 2000 Guineas winner Northern Treasure. The trainer, eighty-three-year-old Kevin Prendergast, again won that race with Awtaad in March 2016.

Also dam of the Italian Oaks heroine Paris Royal, Place D'Etoile has proven to be an international influence. Her descendants have won stakes races in England, Ireland, Italy, South Africa, America and Japan.

Prince Of Penzance is her second descendant to run in the

Melbourne Cup, her great grandson Oscar Schindler finishing fifteenth as favourite behind Saintly in 1996.

And just three months before Prince Of Penzance's Cup victory, another of her descendants in Arabian Queen caused an upset, defeating hot favourite Golden Horn in the Juddmonte International Stakes at York.

It seems this is a family of longshots. At that stage Golden Horn was the undefeated winner of the Epsom and Irish Derby, and he would go on to Prix de l'Arc de Triomphe success. At York he was a 4/9 favourite. Arabian Queen was 50–1.

This family is one that has been producing high achievers for generations. Prince Of Penzance, as his name suggests, boasts royal lineage — he is able to count among his relations the big race winners In The Wings, Dubawi, High Rise, High Hawk, Zomaradah, Virginia Waters, Chachamaidee, Infamy, Fidalgo, Talgo and Chaise.

And another Melbourne Cup runner, Second Coming, who ran third to his stablemate Brew in 2000.

Lots of horses, lots of stories. All part of Prince Of Penzance's Melbourne Cup.

Chapter Seventeen

RICH HILL STUD

CAMERA crews like to get a bit arty on Melbourne Cup Day. Shots from above, from the side, from below. It looks good but can make a race a bit hard to follow. A crucial moment can be missed.

This, however, may add to the excitement rather than detract from it, and such was the case for those watching the 2015 Melbourne Cup from Rich Hill Stud, birthplace of Prince Of Penzance.

The Cup takes place late afternoon Waikato time and Rich Hill's staff got to knock off a little bit early that day. They crowded into the boss John Thompson's lounge room, twenty or so sets of eyes on his big television screen.

It was a nice race to watch for Prince Of Penzance fans. The horse, despite getting his head up a few times early, soon settled into a good rhythm and enjoyed smooth running along the rails.

At the 600 metres Michelle Payne made a move, slight but significant, so quick that if you were blinking at the time you would've missed it.

Watching from New Zealand everyone missed it, the camera angles changing to an on the ground shot, a flurry of hooves on screen, before flashing back to the bigger picture.

And in that split second everything had changed.

'I could see a long way out that he was going well, he was cruising on the fence,' John Thompson recalled, 'then the television flashed to the ground and back. And in that next shot he was out into the clear ... what a great bit of riding!'

It was then that a bit of cheering began at Rich Hill, reaching a crescendo as Prince Of Penzance hit the lead with 200 metres to go.

'We were screaming, the place just went berserk, everyone was so happy.'

A sensation that has not diminished since, Thompson enjoying the Cup's extensive aftermath, from the interviews with television crews who arrived at the farm the next day, to the presentation of the breeder's Melbourne Cup at Ellerslie racetrack in late January.

Michelle Payne was present at the latter, rather apt given that the day's feature, the Karaka Million (New Zealand's richest race), was won for the first time by a female jockey, Danielle Johnson successful aboard Xiong Feng.

As John Thompson collected the miniature version of the iconic trophy (now proudly on display at Rich Hill) on behalf of his co-breeders Alan Galbraith and Jungle Pocket Pty Ltd (Mr Katsumi Yoshida) he had in his mind the journey that took him to that moment, a story with roots in New Zealand and Japan.

It was in 1997 that dual Group One winner Pentire first stepped onto Waikato soil, the Japanese owned stallion shuttling from his northern hemisphere base, the world famous Shadai Farm.

Purchased while still in work as a four-year-old by Teruya Yoshida, Pentire had proven himself in the strongest of company, winning the Irish Champion Stakes and the prestigious King George VI and Queen Elizabeth Diamond Stakes at Royal Ascot.

His acquirement by Shadai was in some quarters rued at the time, English breeders disappointed to be denied the opportunity to breed to the well-credentialled stallion.

A son of highly successful stallion Be My Guest from the family of Epsom and Irish Derby hero Shirley Heights, Pentire may have been a loss to Europe but he was a great gain to Australasia.

While he has been represented by four stakes winners in Japan and another four from a three-year stint at Germany's Gestut Isarland (breeders of Monsun, sire of the Melbourne Cup winners Fiorente and Protectionist), it is in this part of the world that Pentire has shone.

At the time of writing Pentire was the sire of thirty-eight southern hemisphere stakes winners, fourteen of whom have won at the elite level.

Two of his sons have claimed dual New Zealand Horse Of The Year titles, the evergreen Mufhasa and the brilliant but sadly somewhat untapped Xcellent, who provided his sire another moment in Melbourne Cup history when running a gallant third behind Makybe Diva in 2005.

Zarita, Rangirangdoo, Pantani, Say No More, Art Success, Recurring, Pentane, Penny Gem, Ferlax (born just a few weeks before Prince Of Penzance at Rich Hill) and Markus Maximus have also won at the elite level, as has Xtravagant, who just four days after Prince Of Penzance's Melbourne Cup was stunning recording an eight-and-half-length victory in the 2000 Guineas at Riccarton, just out of Christchurch.

Pentire's progeny have amassed over $95 million in stakes. Nobody is prouder of his achievements than John Thompson, who has a definite soft spot for Pentire and his progeny.

'Pentire and his foals are great to deal with,' he said. 'They are so full of energy; they never tire.'

It was that innate vigour that played against Prince Of Penzance at the yearling sales, Thompson recalling that it was no easy task to get him to walk properly in front of potential buyers.

'He was always jig-jogging,' he said, 'and he just didn't show himself off as well as he could have.'

'But he was always an athlete, correct and sound.'

Prince Of Penzance was the seventh foal produced by the

American bred mare Royal Successor, an unraced but regally bred daughter of the legendary Mr Prospector and the dual Yorkshire Oaks winner Only Royale.

After producing little of note in Japan (just the one winner of one race from five foals), Royal Successor arrived in New Zealand via Australia in July 2008. It was the intention that she would be a mate for her owner's stallion Jungle Pocket, who had been shuttling to Rich Hill.

But during the equine influenza outbreak of 2007 the winner of the Japan Derby and Japan Cup was stranded in Victoria for the year. After serving fifty mares, including Royal Successor, he returned to Japan for good.

And so Royal Successor had just the one Jungle Pocket; a gelding called Greystoke who retired a maiden after seventeen starts in Australia and Singapore, her sixth not so successful foal in a row. However, while he was at his mother's side she was served by Pentire, with John Thompson happy for him to step into Jungle Pocket's shoes.

'I suggested that Pentire would be a good fit for Royal Successor as he was doing so well with Mr Prospector line mares,' he said, recalling that Pentire's 'first good horse' Pentastic (a seven times winner of over $1.9 million) was out of a mare by Mr Prospector's son Bellotto, while his dual Group One winning daughter Zarita was also bred on the cross.

'It looked to be a very good match on paper as well as on type, and Mr Yoshida agreed.'

Royal Successor, who died in 2015, was, said John 'a very good bodied mare but not completely correct'.

Well aware that the Mr Prospector breed were not known for their pretty front legs, John knew that Pentire was a stallion able to upgrade his mares.

'He has always been known for siring sound, correct stock, horses who can stand the test of time. So I was confident that he could breed her faults out.'

So happy was he with the mating with Royal Successor that he repeated it several times, the outcomes being the filly Penthouse Princess (lightly raced and showing promise) and a colt sold at the 2016 Karaka sale.

Knocked down to a bid of NZ$200,000 from Penthouse Princess's trainer Henry Dwyer, he is described by John as 'a different type to Prince Of Penzance, more forward physically with a bit more quality, more of a miler type than a stayer.'

While John does not have any specific memory of the birth of Prince Of Penzance — he is, after all, present at around a hundred foalings each spring — he does however still have the notes he recorded in the stud's annual foaling sheet.

'A quality, athletic colt.'

Just four words, but he was spot-on!

Though the market at the 2011 New Zealand Bloodstock Premier Yearling Sale did not necessarily agree, the Pentire colt sold early (lot 22) on day one as buyers were still testing the waters.

'We had some very nice Pentires go through the ring that year,' John recalled, 'including Ferlax [future Australian Guineas winner] and a few people were hanging off waiting for him.'

'I think if Prince Of Penzance had been in later he would've sold better,' John said, adding that the colt's late November foaling date had also worked against him — 'He was just that bit immature.'

Originally passed in for NZ$40,000 and sold just minutes later to John Foote for $50,000, Prince Of Penzance was one of the cheapest Pentires sold in 2011, that year seeing eighteen of his progeny fetching six-figure sums at various sales. This included the $520,000 colt who would race as Entirely Platinum, winner of the 2014 Sky High Stakes at Rosehill.

Prince Of Penzance's bargain price tag is one of the reasons, said John, that the horse has captured the attention of so many in both New Zealand and Australia.

'He has made people feel that the Melbourne Cup dream is still possible — that you don't have to be a Sheikh or a millionaire. His win changed everyone's perception of a race that had been dominated for several years by the northern hemisphere.'

It had been eight years (Zabeel's son Efficient in 2007) since a horse bred in New Zealand had won the Melbourne Cup, a race the country had enjoyed so much success in throughout its 154-year history.

'Prince Of Penzance continued the rich history that New Zealand bred horses have in the Melbourne Cup,' said New Zealand Bloodstock's Managing Director, Andrew Seabrook.

'Watching the race unfold was just incredible. We were thrilled for Rich Hill, for John Foote and delighted to see Michelle — who has Kiwi bloodlines — make history,' he said. 'There is something about the Melbourne Cup that just sets it apart; it is the pinnacle of Australasian racing.'

'It was like going back in time to when New Zealand was regularly winning the Cup,' John Thompson said, adding that, 'we took it a bit for granted.'

For decades there was a friendly Australia/New Zealand rivalry, but in 2015 it was as though the two countries were united, John noting that he was 'overwhelmed by all the congratulations from Australia.'

And of course by the many well-wishers closer to home, John noting that the Melbourne Cup is New Zealand's favourite race.

'It should actually be called the race that stops two nations,' John said. 'It is New Zealand's biggest betting race; every office has a sweep, the once-a-year bettors come out of the woodwork and horses like Kiwi are legends here. So for us to win it — it meant a lot, a huge thrill, not only for us but for the whole of New Zealand.

'It is something no-one can ever take away. I can die a happy man, not any time soon though, knowing I've bred a Melbourne Cup winner!'

Hoofnote: Both John Thompson and Katsumi Yoshida boast further links to the Melbourne Cup, Rich Hill Stud standing the 2009 winner Shocking, while Shadai's Northern Farm bred the 2006 quinella of Delta Blues and Pop Rock.

Chapter Eighteen

JOHN FOOTE

IT was a relaxed Melbourne Cup Day for bloodstock agent John Foote. His work was done, the ground work, that is — the in-depth study of a yearling sale catalogue, the time spent at Karaka inspecting every young horse and re-inspecting those who took his fancy.

And a third look at those he really liked, such as lot 22 at the 2011 New Zealand Bloodstock Premier Yearling Sale. A bay colt not really typical of his sire Pentire — 'Not quite as pretty as a lot of them are. He was a tough-looking yearling. There was a lot of Mr Prospector [his dam's sire] about him and he moved very well.'

'Okay walker' is pretty much all it says in John's notes in his catalogue, though he explains that it is actually a compliment. 'I don't write a lot down and my friends will tell you that "okay" means I like the horse.'

And so the 'not overly big' colt made it to John's final list. But he did not actually bid, assuming that a good type with a strong pedigree would fetch around $100,000, more than he was inclined to spend, especially as he didn't have a specific order for the horse.

Often an agent will go to sale looking for a particular type of horse for a particular client, but John's relationship with Darren Weir has always been a little different.

'Darren is always on the lookout for a nice middle distance type and I had bought a Pentire for him before. He doesn't ask me to buy any one horse, but I know that if I see one he'd like he would be happy to take it on.'

The Pentire colt was not a horse John would typically promote to the top of his list. He passed conformation criteria, but there was a concern about the record of his dam, the American mare Royal Successor, imported from Japan.

'This is her seventh foal,' read the catalogue page, 'dam of three foals to race … one winner.'

Not an imposing record, and John had circled it in his catalogue.

'Normally that would put me off, but I had noticed that Rich Hill Stud had been enjoying success with mares from Japan who had been previously disappointing. So I was not as worried as I normally would've been.'

The bidding for lot 22 was not vigorous, reaching only NZ$40,000, and he was passed in having failed to reach the reserve of $50,000.

Luckily for John he happened to be in the ring at the time, recalling that he 'could not believe' the young horse was not sold.

'So I rushed around to his stable where [Rich Hill Stud's] John Thompson was in shock. He thought he had an $80,000 and up sort of horse. I rang Darren, he agreed to buy him for $50,000, so John and I shook hands on it.'

Fast forward four years later and John was watching Flemington from afar, enjoying the day's racing on television with his wife via a holiday home on the Sunshine Coast.

There was a level of anxiety, John quietly confident that the horse would run well having spoken to Darren Weir a few days previously.

'He thought he would finish in the top ten, but I thought he was an even better chance than that,' he said, adding that while he does not often bet, he did 'have a little each-way going'.

'He was crazy odds after his run in the Moonee Valley Cup. He got fired up in that race after a horse sat outside him and Michelle was forced to take off a fair way from home. He was grabbed close to the line and they broke the track record. It was a phenomenal run. The winner of that race [The United States] was 20–1 in the Cup and Prince Of Penzance was 100–1. It didn't make sense.'

There was movement in the Foote household as the Melbourne Cup was run. He recalls starting on the couch but edging closer and closer to the television as the race unfolded.

And as he did so he was noticing just how well Prince Of Penzance was travelling. 'He was bolting, and when Michelle got him off the fence and into clear running it was fantastic!'

'By the time he had crossed the line we were very close to the TV set,' John laughed, recalling the feeling of exhilaration of the win. 'We jumped up and down; we were very happy!'

'It is the epitome of what I do,' he explained. 'I don't go to the sales looking to spend large amounts of money; I look for the value, and that is what Prince Of Penzance was.'

In his exuberant post-race interview with Channel 7 Darren Weir had many people to thank, but one of the first was the man who bought the horse — 'What a great judge John Foote is,' he enthused.

John had experienced that Melbourne Cup thrill before, in fact an amazing three times before.

For, in 1998, he purchased for 60,000 guineas at the Tattersalls December Sale the lightly raced Tugela in foal to Danehill's Irish Derby winning son Desert King.

The foal inside her went through the ring, but was another fortunate passed in story. After failing to reach her reserve she was retained by John's client Tony Santic, who christened her Makybe Diva. As the cliché goes, the rest is history!

Chapter Nineteen

ANZAC LODGE

IT was 'an immature little horse' who arrived at Dean Hawthorne's Anzac Lodge in early February 2011.

Along with a number of other graduates of the Karaka Yearling Sale Series he had been floated the 120 kilometres south from Auckland to Cambridge, to begin the slow and steady process of becoming a racehorse.

The first couple of months were just a matter of rest and recreation, playing with a mate. Dean noticed that two of the colts trusted to his care had the same Rich Hill Stud brand, so he paired them up.

'I thought they had probably been running together as weanlings so it seemed a good idea to keep them together.'

Fast forward a few years and Dean wishes he had taken a photo of the friends in their paddock. Both sons of Pentire, both Group One winners — Prince Of Penzance and Ferlax.

After a couple of months, it was time for the education to begin, the individual needs of each horse to be taken into consideration.

There is no point rushing a horse not ready for the challenges he faces. Some are natural get-up-and-go youngsters, cocky and ready to take on the world.

Others are not so sure of themselves, and they need that bit of time, that bit of help to grow into their bodies and their minds.

It is a matter of obtaining the balance of pressure. Enough on them to encourage growth and maturity, not so much that they go sour and resentful.

Dean's methods are similar to so many others in New Zealand, land of the patient horseman.

The young horses under his care are put through a process, a period of breaking followed by rest, then back in for further education.

Out again, in again. Out and in — as many times as it takes.

This relaxed approach is good for the equine body and mind. They can develop at their own pace. If they are ready early well and good, if not time is their friend.

Prince Of Penzance was one of those who needed time. And quite a bit of it, with the first course of his breaking in period a short one.

'He was a backward little horse who just wasn't coping,' Dean recalled, 'so we had to back off and give him another couple of months.'

Sam Beatson, a breaker who was working with Dean, was happy with him next time around, though there were no early pointers to future stardom.

'I would like to say that he was a stand-out to break in,' he laughed. 'But he was just a nice, straightforward horse who went through the routine and did all that was asked of him. He had a good attitude and moved well with good balance.'

Through the New Zealand winter Prince Of Penzance just pottered around, enjoying the rich Cambridge grass. A little fright one day, a mild case of colic, but all was well.

But it was not until the emergence of spring that he 'started to thrive and thicken up'.

All up, Prince Of Penzance remained in New Zealand for around a year after his purchase by John Foote. He left Anzac Lodge in the summer, bound for Ballarat.

Did he create a startling first impression? No, says Darren Weir. 'He was one of many young horses, no stand-out.'

Well, not yet.

Part Three

THE PLAYERS

'It is the horse people who fit in best.'

Chapter Twenty

DARREN WEIR

IT was not a rare occurrence for a four-year-old Darren Weir to go walk-about from the family home at Berriwillock in Victoria's wheat growing Mallee district.

His mother Noelene didn't panic; she knew exactly where he would be.

'He used to disappear all the time,' she laughed, 'but I knew where he was … up the road where there were ponies. I'd always find him on a horse.'

Despite the fact that the Weir family had no particular interest in the equine, Darren was born with a love of the horse.

While he was never very happy at school — 'it just wasn't his forte' — Darren was at his most content on horseback, keenly participating in local pony club activities.

Described by Noelene as a typical young boy — 'No bloody angel!' — Darren learned much from his first horse, a tricky palomino by the name of Sonny.

'Sonny was too good for him at the start,' Darren's father Roy told the *Herald Sun*'s Matt Stewart, 'but he soon got the better of him and after a while he could make that horse do anything … he can make any horse do anything.'

Berriwillock local Bobby Borlase remembers Darren hanging

with his mates, listening to music. Much like every other youngster, though with a difference.

'He was the cheeky kid on the horse,' he said, 'and when other kids moved on to motorbikes Darren stayed on the horse.'

And it did not take Darren long to realise that he wanted to make horses his life. He just had to pluck up the courage to tell his mum.

'What will there be in racing for him?' she asked Jack Coffey, who was with Darren when he announced that school was not for him.

He told her that he wished to work full-time for Jack, a trainer at nearby Birchip.

Jack laughs at the memory of that Friday evening, one where he was keen to get away from the Weir home as quickly as possible!

'It was the last thing she said to me that night,' he said, remembering Noelene's less-than-enthusiastic response to her son's news. 'She went berserk, as any mother would. She just wanted the best possible education for him.'

When Jack left the argument was not yet settled, but Darren would get his way. Soon afterwards the 'young skinny kid' was at Jack's making an immediate impression.

'He had that bit of shyness and didn't yet have the confidence to look people in the eye. But he was already a more than capable rider and he had a great attitude to his work.'

Beginning what would be a lifelong friendship with Jack's younger brother Austy, Darren quickly settled into a varied life working with racehorses, broodmares and stallions.

'He was doing everything from holding mares while they were being served, to carting hay and other farm jobs. Right from the start he was willing to learn, and learn he did.'

Jack and his late wife Sandra didn't have a son but Darren, who at times lived with them, became a treasured family member.

And he is still very close to John Castleman, the Mildura trainer who Darren gained further experience with.

John remembers Darren standing out from other young men who came to work for him. 'So many of them wanted to just tell you how good they were, but with Darren you hardly even knew he was there. He would just get on with his work, he was always on the move.'

'You only ever had to tell him something once,' John said, recognising ambition in Darren from the start. 'He wanted to be something.'

After stints with Colin Hayes at Lindsay Park and at a stable in Ireland, Darren moved to Stawell where he worked both as a farrier and breaker, spending a number of years with trainer Terry O'Sullivan, who was also impressed by his attitude.

'Not many people work like he does,' he said, chuckling at the memory of Darren turning up to the stables on day one on top of one horse, holding another. His truck had broken down six or so kilometres out of Stawell so he rode bareback into town.

Then there was the day Darren, while playing football for Stawell, broke his leg. He had promised to build yards for another trainer and was not going to renege, so there he was, working hard, undeterred by having one leg in plaster.

When land across the road became available, the O'Sullivans helped Darren out financially. Having noticed that he painted his stables maroon and white, Robyn O'Sullivan thought of the perfect twenty-first birthday present for him — his own set of silks in those colours.

Taking out an owner/trainer licence in 1995, Darren didn't take long to get into the winner's stall, his mare Epaulay at just her second start racing away with an Avoca maiden on Caulfield Cup Day, 21 October.

Two years later Darren was a fully licensed trainer, and in 2001 he relocated to Ballarat, purchasing stables built by Lloyd Williams for local legend Noel Kelly.

One of his earliest and most significant winners from his new Forest Lodge base was an Archway filly called She's Archie. Closely related to his first winner Epaulay, she easily won a Horsham maiden at her third start in December 2001, and in May the following year became his first Group One winner when taking out the South Australian Oaks at Morphettville.

Because of that win, and because of his burgeoning reputation as a hardworking skilled horseman, Darren's ownership base began to expand.

One keen racehorse owner and breeder, St Kilda Football Club's Hall Of Famer Stuart Trott, noticed Darren early. 'I would just watch him at the races and he was doing everything. He was one of the hardest-working blokes I had ever seen.'

Stuart had a nice horse in his paddock and was on the lookout for a trainer. He invited Darren over for lunch and a chat, and played hard-ball. He'd had a couple of negative experiences in the past, trainers who had said one thing, done another.

'I said so long as he never lied to me I'd stick with him — and he never has. He is just an honest, straight-shooting bloke; a good Aussie lad.'

Having shown ability, the horse in the paddock was christened Baldock after Darrel Baldock, who in 1966 became the first and only captain to lead St Kilda to a premiership victory.

Missing the start at debut, Baldock finished a game second but was able to atone for that defeat by winning five races, including four in a row in the winter of 2002.

Stuart has always been impressed by Darren's no-fuss attitude to training horses. He doesn't string owners along, he doesn't persevere with the hopeless — 'He has sacked more of mine than he has trained,' Stuart laughed.

'This kid can train,' Stuart said one day to mate Gerry Ryan, who heeded his advice to send Darren a horse, thus becoming his first high-profile owner.

One of the first to notice the talent of champion footballer Tony Lockett, Stuart jokes that 'he spotted the equivalent in the horse world'.

Stuart also recommended Darren to Ed and Robyn Shakespeare, fellow members of an informal group of thoroughbred breeding enthusiasts who have met once a month for a couple of decades to discuss all things racing.

'Ed said he had a paddock full of horses, but he couldn't get anyone to come and look at them. I said Darren would.'

Which he did, and Robyn remembers the day. 'He said if we were happy to move on horses who he thought would not make it he would train for us. He wanted to win and we said that's what we want too. We've been together ever since.'

In November 2003, Darren was represented by his first Melbourne Cup runner, the South Australian Oaks winner She's Archie. Twice threatened by serious bouts of colic, she was a gallant second to Makybe Diva in the first of that great mare's historic treble.

He told *The Age*'s Andrew Eddy that he had 'never been so happy to run second'.

'I never knew that getting beaten could feel so good. She ran a great race and I am so proud of her.'

That same season saw Darren represented by a hundred winners for the first time, and since 2005 he has been Victoria's leading country trainer. Nine years running he has had over a hundred winners per season. His stable's growth over the last three seasons has been staggering, with 253 winners in 2013/14 (the season he became the first solely country-based trainer to win the metropolitan premiership, ending a three-year Peter Moody reign) and 286 in 2014/15.

And at Moonee Valley on 13 July 2016, he broke the Commonwealth record of 334 winners set by John Hawkes in 2002/03.

Not that it was all that important to him, Darren shaking off a club official who wanted him to celebrate with an exploding bottle of champagne.

His website proudly lists, in order of number of wins, the stable's highest achieving horses. It is by no means a dry statistical table, as each horse's name is accompanied in brackets by their stable name … Gotta Take Care, the winner of twenty races, is Woody; Puissance de Lune is Frenchy; Prince Of Penzance is, aptly, Success.

There have, of course, been setbacks to Darren's career. Some controversy here and there, suspensions, fines. But he has always fought back, with those loyal to the stable sticking solidly.

He is by no means an extrovert, but he isn't quite the introvert either, as Terry O'Sullivan said, 'He is the hardest of workers but he doesn't mind a party either.'

He recognises his own weaknesses and seeks to rectify them, hiring racing owners' services and financial managers to oversee the parts of the business he doesn't enjoy. That way he can concentrate on what matters most to him.

'I like the horses and the staff who work with them, but the rest of it I'm not good at,' he told the *Courier Mail*'s Tim O'Connor in July 2014.

Meeting Darren when fulfilling his role as treasurer at the Ballarat Turf Club, Michael Leonard was at first racing manager for the stables, taking a year off before returning as financial manager, bringing with him Luke Archibald, account manager.

Previously running his own accountancy firm, Michael is a long-term lover of the horse. He operates Millwater Agistment Farm, where a number of the stable horses — including, at one stage, Prince Of Penzance — spell.

'Darren is very easy to get on with,' Michael says — and good to work for. 'He wants to know everything about everything, but once he trusts you he leaves you to get on with it. He likes to be informed on every aspect of the business but is not controlling or dominating with it.

'When you make a mistake, and we all do, he lets you know but that is the end of it — there is no blame. Though if someone is not pulling their weight or keeps making the same mistakes, there is no place for them.

'He has a knack for making people feel that they are integral to his success, something that generates a lot of loyalty. That is why nearly all his key people are also his mates.'

That loyalty extends to his owners (he has over 2300 of them), Darren struck with a feeling of guilt if a horse is too slow to race, often offering to put them into a horse of his own showing ability.

He takes training seriously, but not himself. 'He can take the mickey out of himself,' Michael said. 'Success has not altered him.'

And he works hard and long, an office set aside for him used so rarely that it was allotted to someone else — 'I think he only sat in that chair twice,' Michael laughed.

Much of Darren's work is done at the races or to and from the races. He was once seen at an agistment farm at 7.30pm on a Saturday in his race day suit inspecting horses. This is a life, not a job.

Michael admits to being somewhat in awe of his boss and friend. 'I have long been fascinated as to what makes successful people … what makes a Darren Weir? He has an amazing decision-making capability, the ability to quickly get the point.'

Prince Of Penzance owner and long-time stable supporter John Richards agrees. 'Darren can clear his mind of anything that is not relevant. And he doesn't stew over anything that is irreversible.'

A respect of other's opinions is also present, John joking that he doesn't always see eye-to-eye with his trainer and friend. 'We *often* disagree about horses,' he laughs.

Darren also has, says Michael, 'charisma, the X-factor'.

Not that the media and general racing public see that side of him too often. At the races, even after winning the Melbourne Cup, he is keen to deflect attention.

In his interviews with Channel 7 after Prince Of Penzance's

victory he doesn't talk about himself; he thanks everyone he can think of.

And he doesn't revel in the hype.

'He hates it,' John Richards says. 'He is getting used to it, but it doesn't mean he enjoys it!'

Race caller Greg Miles notices this as well. 'Darren Weir is very comfortable flying under the radar,' he laughs.

Michael was amazed at Darren's calmness on Melbourne Cup morning. He was in the office as usual, discussing business matters. 'He may have been nervous, but he didn't show it. It was just another working day.'

Sometimes in charge of a large stable, a trainer becomes more management than hands-on. But that will never be Darren Weir.

He still, for example, does much of the work training young horses how to cope with the barrier stalls. Sometimes this is dangerous — horses are not naturally keen on enclosed spaces and they don't enjoy the feeling of steel on their flanks.

Michael one day suggested to Darren that he should no longer undertake such a risky task. His reply: 'The day I can't do this anymore is the day I stop training horses.'

The horses at Forest Lodge are treated as individuals, each allotted a track rider who will suit their personality, each homed in the stable or paddock that makes them happiest.

'We can all pick what is wrong with a horse, but Darren has the gift to see what is right,' Michael said, adding that for each horse, 'he gives hugely specific instructions'.

'I have tried to figure out what it is that makes him such a great trainer, but it is so hard. There is that degree of intelligence and science, but it is also intuition. People have in the past tried to copy Bart Cummings or T. J. Smith but they can't.'

Darren loves horses, fears snakes and heights. He cannot bear disloyalty; the opposite is treasured.

'He prizes and rewards loyalty,' Michael said.

Michael has at times considered retirement, but he knows it is not for him — and Darren knows it too.

'When I win a Blue Diamond or a Golden Slipper you can retire,' Darren jokes. The chances of him pushing a two-year-old towards those early goals are as likely as the Melbourne Cup being changed to a 1000-metre race run at Seymour.

'He is extremely patient and puts a lot of work into making horses relax, to get them to switch off.'

Formerly public relations manager at Waikato Stud, New Zealand, Jeremy Rogers is racing manager, part of the team for six years. His father was a racing journalist so he was born into the game, and he always wanted to be a part of it.

'Early on I thought of being a stockbroker, but only so as to make enough money to own racehorses!'

Having been at the 2011 Karaka sales, Jeremy was one of the first from the stables to lay eyes on Prince Of Penzance, remembering that 'for a little horse he had a massive walk'.

Jeremy's job was already busy prior to Prince Of Penzance's Melbourne Cup victory and things certainly have not slackened off with the stable's ownership base widening. 'We are training for Sheikhs now!'

Jeremy has watched his boss at work and cannot help but admire the way he has with his animals.

'Horses do for him what they will do for nobody else. That is the first thing you notice about him — he is a true horseman and he has a brilliant mind.'

And once a horse is in that brilliant mind, it does not leave.

'He will see a slow horse he trained a few years before and know who it is. But he is hopeless with people's names — often at the races he will nudge me and ask, "Who's that again?"'

Darren's Ballarat stables (sometimes fondly referred to as 'Weir Town') have grown and grown over the years, many of its owner's profits put into improvements. Everything a horse could ask for is there: paddocks, spacious stables, a pool, two walking machines, indoor and outdoor riding arenas, a couple of undercover treadmills and hyperbaric facilities.

Each of the laneways connecting paddocks and stables are named after horses … Skewiff Lane, Leica Ding Lane, True Courser Lane, She's Archie Lane.

The Ballarat track is within walking distance, as is the club's 1400-metre uphill synthetic track, which enables horses to gain in strength and power without putting undue pressure on their joints.

Then there are the Warrnambool stables, shared with local trainer Matthew Williams. Always immaculate, always peaceful, they are close to the beach with its sand dunes and soothing waters.

Weir employs a staff of a hundred (seventy full time), nine of whom are in the office, one built only recently but already proving too small!

Angela Taylor-Moy, with Darren almost since the start, is a foreperson, as is Johnno Bower who rarely leaves his station from 4am to noon, overseeing and coordinating the hundred or so horses heading out to work each morning.

These are not your average nine-to-five workers. They love racing and are passionate about their jobs, and even those in charge of paperwork are involved in the sport … 'It is the horse people who fit in best.'

Chapter Twenty-One

MICHELLE PAYNE

WITH its two handles signifying unity, the Loving Cup is a traditional vessel passed around at weddings and banquets. It has a lengthy history, one that long predates the first running of the Melbourne Cup in 1861.

Its history is one of Celtic, Irish, French and Jewish roots. But in Australia it took its own special form when, in 1919 James Steeth added his own twist to tradition.

Commissioned, via Drummonds Jewellers, by the Victoria Racing Club to 'design a trophy that would be in keeping with the prestige of the race', Steeth added a third handle to a historic trophy, and the modern-day Melbourne Cup was born.

It had been, says the VRC's Cup Tour Manager Joe McGrath, a work in progress, with the 1916 trophy won by Sasanof consisting of a bowl and handles without the stem and base.

'Gradually it evolved into the trophy we see today,' he said, noting that there have been some minor changes along the way, with a gold tax imposed by the government in the 1930s seeing the size of the bowl shrink a little.

It was not until Americain's win in 2010 that it returned to its previous fuller size.

The 1915 trophy won by Patrobas was the last one made in the

United Kingdom. It very nearly did not make it to Flemington, its progress across the oceans impeded by World War I. The VRC did not want to risk the 1916 winner leaving the course empty-handed and decided from thereon that it should be made locally.

Despite the fact that it was wartime, the press paid close attention to the new Melbourne Cup. The pressure was on the VRC to get it exactly right.

Which they and James Steeth did.

Instead of those two handles symbolising the relationship between husband and wife, the bringing together of two families, there were three … one each for the winning jockey, trainer and owner of Australia's most prestigious horse race.

Two of those three handles have in the past signified women. A hundred years before Prince Of Penzance won the big race it was taken out by Edith Widdis's Patrobas. She was recognised as the first female owner of a Melbourne Cup winner. Coincidentally, Patrobas also wore the number 19 saddle cloth.

There has been, over the years, conjecture that Edith Widdis may also have been the trainer at a time when licences were granted only to men. It was not until 2001 that the first official female Melbourne Cup winning trainer was celebrated: Sheila Laxon with Ethereal.

That just left the jockey's handle. And that honour would go to Michelle Payne.

◆ ◆ ◆

There is wonderful footage of a baby-faced Michelle Payne being interviewed by a television program a couple of decades ago. She was around nine or so, and was being asked of her ambitions.

'I just want to win the Melbourne Cup.'

Some great jockeys have held the same dream; actually, they all do. But not all get to fulfil it, including some of Australia's best. There are few more skilled hands than Darren Gauci's. He hasn't won it.

Neither did Michelle Payne's high-achieving brother Patrick.

And for a few years now the Melbourne Cup has been an aim internationally. The world's most famous rider, Frankie Dettori, has had fourteen attempts, twice running second.

A jockey needs a lot of luck to win it, to be on the right horse at the right time. But it is a race that asks of its participants professionalism, skill, calmness.

Michelle Payne embodies each of those qualities. She was remarkably serene in the lead up, surprising even herself.

'I woke up this morning,' she told ABC program *7.30* from Flemington that night, 'and I was as calm as anything, I couldn't believe how good I felt.'

In owner Darren Lonsdale's pre-race recording on Melbourne Cup Day she talks about her plans for the race in such a laidback style that it could be a maiden at Terang, not a $6 million event with the world's racing eyes watching.

She took that composure into the race, something Prince Of Penzance undoubtedly picked up on. And she earned worldwide admiration with the rawness and honesty of her post-race comments televised on Channel 7, firstly thanking Darren Weir and those loyal to her, before commenting that 'women can do anything, and we can beat the world!'

Comments made by her regarding some owners wanting a change were played up by the media, but it was, Sandy McGregor said, never really a big deal.

In every horse with multiple owners there are differences of opinion, especially regarding who rides. There were times when one or two of Prince Of Penzance's connections thought that maybe someone else would suit, but it was not a major issue — as evidenced by the fact that Michelle missed only one ride on him, a day on which she was suspended.

'There has never been any real discussion about her not riding,' Sandy said, 'just a little bit of noise.'

Sandy is one of many preferring to recognise Michelle for her talents and her amazing story rather than her femaleness. 'I think the gender angle has been a bit overplayed,' he said.

Michelle was inclined to agree. When asked by a reporter what it was like to be the first female rider of a Melbourne Cup winner she said that despite her initial outburst among the euphoria it had not been uppermost in her thoughts.

'I don't really see the significance that much, but I hope it helps female jockeys.'

Other riders agreed, Libby Hopwood writing in South Australian newspaper *The Advertiser* a couple of days later that 'a female jockey winning the Melbourne Cup was bound to happen'.

'The congratulations for Michelle winning the Cup should be for being a great rider who gave her horse a fabulous ride, rather than because she's female,' Libby said.

'Michelle is a hardworking woman who has overcome serious injuries and fought back to hone her art and flourish in a sport she loves,' she continued, adding, 'I can't wait for the future of racing when the sex of the jockey is not a consideration for trainers and owners ... when [they are selected] on merit instead of whether they sit down to use the toilet.'

What is more important than the gender or even the talent of the jockey, Sandy McGregor says, is the rider/horse relationship. A regular partnership fosters familiarity and mutual esteem.

'Having the same jockey every start makes a difference; you get more consistent results. They have to know the horse. It is not like jumping on a motorbike.'

And there is no doubt that Michelle loves Prince Of Penzance, keen to see that his effort as well as hers was recognised.

'I've got so much respect for him because he is so tough,' she said in a post-race interview. 'I thought if ever a horse is going to win the Melbourne Cup, it is going to be him.'

'I know the inner strength that he has,' she continued. 'What he has done in some of the races, even when he hasn't won … to finish off like he does, I think this horse is incredible.'

Owner Mark Hall recognises the relationship between horse and jockey, and the time and effort Michelle has put into fostering it.

'One day we watched her ride Prince Of Penzance in track work at Terang. From there she went to ride at Bendigo and later that night at Moonee Valley. She has put in enormous miles for this horse.'

Prince Of Penzance's strapper Maddie Raymond also applauds the admiration Michelle has for the horse.

'She knows that horse, every little bit about him. She loves him as much as anyone else. I'd struggle to find a better jockey for Prince Of Penzance.'

Bruce Dalton agrees: 'She may not be the best jockey in Australia, but she is the best jockey for our horse — she knows him and he knows her.'

Another owner, Sam Brown, said that he and his fellow members of the Men In Hats Syndicate 'loved Michelle from day one'.

'She is such a warm, friendly and positive person. She is a delight, always happy to speak with us.

'We knew female jockeys could get the rough end of the stick, so we thought it was great having Michelle on our team. She added an underdog element to the story, and helped us with our wives and girlfriends — they loved seeing a female jockey have success in a male-dominated sport.'

'We were so happy for Michelle,' he said after the Melbourne Cup. 'She had great faith in the horse from day one, and she truly deserved all the accolades for her hard work and effort. What a ride it was, in the biggest race on the biggest stage. She and the Prince were made for each other.'

'Always modest, always well-spoken,' says another owner, Andrew Broadfoot, of Michelle.

'Our kids admire her; they look up to her,' he added, his wife

Kim agreeing. 'She has been such an inspiration for our girls.'

Not just because of one day, one success, however amazing. But 'because she is such a strong woman.'

The story of where Michelle got that strength, the story of the Payne family, is well documented, both in Tony Kneebone's excellent 1996 book *The Paynes: The Struggle, The Pain, The Glory* and in Michelle's own story *Life As I Know It*.

How she is the youngest of ten children for Paddy and Mary Payne, how her mother was so very tragically killed in a car accident when her last born was a mere six months old.

How seven of her brothers and sisters became jockeys with mixed fortunes, Paddy becoming part of history partnering the champion Northerly in the 2002 W. S. Cox Plate, while in 2007 Bridget, like her mother, died far too young after suffering from injuries sustained in a track work fall.

How she bonded early with her brother Stevie, whose family would not let the fact that he has Down syndrome shape his life.

How in 2014, aged eighteen, she incurred a fractured skull and dangerous bruising to her brain from a fall at Sandown, cared for by her dedicated sisters during a lengthy period of recuperation.

How it was the legendary Bart Cummings who was the first to provide Michelle with a Group One victory (Allez Wonder, 2009 Toorak Handicap) and a Melbourne Cup ride; the same horse three and a half weeks later.

Michelle's first memories, she told ABC's Leigh Sales the day after the Melbourne Cup, revolve around horses. A Shetland pony she was thrown off aged four, her father Paddy insisting she get straight back on.

She recalled watching her siblings ride in races and she knew early that's what she wanted to do as well.

By the time she was fifteen she had left school and not long after she was riding her first winner, Reigning, for her father at her local track, Ballarat.

She admits that it took some time for her to hone her skills, but that's the same for any jockey. But she kept at it, kept improving. And she was rewarded.

◆ ◆ ◆

The Melbourne Cup aftermath was more hectic for Michelle Payne than anyone. While Darren Weir got back to work pretty quickly, while the owners basked in the glory, she was combining a rush of media commitments with her riding.

The day after she had rides on Kyneton Cup Day. She arrived by helicopter and was greeted with applause. 'I feel a bit like a movie star,' she joked to Channel 7, 'it's been a whirlwind.'

That day she spoke fondly of childhood moments spent with Stevie watching their favourite movie over and over … naturally it was *Phar Lap*.

The following Saturday she was again in the winner's circle at Flemington, successful in Listed company aboard the Darren Weir trained Palentino.

And from then on the Melbourne Cup show rolled on.

Shortly after the big race Michelle was named as an ambassador for the Ballarat Cup. The following month she was shortlisted as a finalist for the *Financial Times*' Women Of 2015, while V/Line named their newest train after her, hosting an unveiling at Ballarat Station.

In late January *The Australian* newspaper named her their Australian Of The Year. That same week she took her father back to his country of birth, New Zealand, where she had rides at the Wellington Cup and Karaka Million meetings. While there she headed out to the yearling sales to have a quick cuddle with Prince Of Penzance's yearling brother.

In February she was crowned Ballarat Sportsperson Of The Year, and come March she was still signing autographs and posing for photographs, this time as a special guest at a Rosehill meeting in Sydney.

That same month she and Stevie were crowned the Queen and King Of Moomba, Michelle interviewed by Channel 7 as their float made its way down St Kilda Road.

'It feels pretty special to be up here,' Michelle said, as Stevie enthusiastically waved and bowed to the crowd.

'Stevie is absolutely loving it!' she laughed. 'I think he was made for this.'

'Who would've thought we would be sitting up here as King and Queen,' she said. 'It is an unbelievable experience. It is just amazing, everything that has come along since the Cup win. We could not be more grateful. We are taking it all in and enjoying every moment.'

Later that day Michelle rode at Moonee Valley, Stevie also heading to the track still wearing his Moomba crown.

Then there were invitations to the red carpet screening of *Eddie The Eagle*, Stevie snapped shaking hands with Hugh Jackman while Rachel Griffiths was discussing making a Michelle Payne movie.

In April, Michelle was on the front cover of *Cosmopolitan* for their 'wonder women' issue. And she was on Channel 10's *The Project*, discussing what a great time her brother had been having. 'It was like he was made to be famous!' she joked.

By then she'd met Roger Federer (a moment she described on Twitter as 'maybe the second-best moment of my life' — #starstruck!), Prince Charles and Camilla, and other dignitaries and celebrities.

In May she was at Warrnambool Carnival, signing copies of her book. She was having an amazing time, and there was more to come, with an invitation to ride against international jockeys in the Shergar Cup at Ascot, England, in August.

But sadly she was unable to fulfil that engagement, spending a fortnight in hospital after sustaining internal injuries after a fall at Mildura in May. The media coverage was intense, questions regarding whether she would ride again fired at her. She just wanted time to recover, to consider her future in her own time, at her own pace.

In July Michelle, having purchased a property adjacent to her father's, was among the first to lodge an application for the newly created Victorian dual jockey/trainer licence.

Whatever the future holds for her, whatever successes lie ahead, Michelle Payne will forever be known above all as one thing and it must sit well with her.

'Melbourne Cup winning jockey. I have heard that so many times,' she said. 'I will never get sick of that!'

Chapter Twenty-Two

MADDIE RAYMOND

WARRNAMBOOL'S shipwreck-strewn Lady Bay beach, Friday, 30 October 2015. As far removed from the hustle that is Flemington on Melbourne Cup Day as can be. Just the surf and the sand. A woman and her horse.

Prince Of Penzance's strapper and best friend Maddie Raymond is aboard. Normally she saves him for last; it gives her something to look forward to as she makes her way through her busy morning.

But on this day Prince Of Penzance is in action bright and early, the more time he had back at home resting before the upcoming Tuesday the better. So it was still mostly dark. Just a glimpse of an emerging spring sun, accompanied by the crash of waves.

And Maddie and Prince Of Penzance, the horse she calls Success.

In front of the others on their own. The bond between horse and rider was already strong, they'd done this many times before. She knows him, he knows her. But this was not just any morning, this was Maddie's final ride on Prince Of Penzance before the Melbourne Cup.

Every final ride prior to a race, Maddie says, is nerve-racking. 'You never know if it is going to be the last time. In any race there is a chance of injury and retirement.'

So those usual nerves were there, coupled with extreme

excitement. Not just because Cup Day was looming, but because Prince Of Penzance felt so good, so powerful, that Maddie actually shed a tear as she rode.

'He gave me a phenomenal feel. I knew he was ready.'

And nobody knows this horse as well as Maddie, a horse she refers to as her husband. From the first time she rode him she could feel a shared affection, a mutual respect.

'He loves what he does and I love what I do, it is what we have in common.'

It was Prince Of Penzance's toughness that first appealed to Maddie, a quality she has always admired. A very smart horse, one with a big heart. And lots of personality.

'He is very playful. He does not have a nasty bone in his body, but he likes to think he is top dog. He knew from the start that he was good.'

Prince Of Penzance quite likes a game. He and his Group One winning stablemate, Stratum Star, have made up one of their own. Stratum Star pokes his tongue out, Prince Of Penzance grabs it. They do this over and over.

Prince Of Penzance has a bit of a sweet tooth, and he loves the particularly succulent top half of carrots. Maddie more often than not has one in her pocket and when she approaches that is where he heads first. She doesn't even have to hand it to him.

He is a fearless horse; he would run towards something frightening rather than away from it. This helps with the training of younger horses — if one needs a bit of soothing, a bit of coaxing, Prince Of Penzance is the man for the job.

Sometimes locals walk their dogs at Lady Bay and they can stir horses up. They run around, barking. Prince Of Penzance isn't bothered and helps calm his stablemates who are.

He generally prefers to be worked on his own. Such is his competitive nature that galloping with others tends to fire him up a bit.

Maddie likes this alone time. Her fellow workers know not to disturb her during this perfect forty minutes or so. Before the Melbourne Cup it was time just to let her mind wander into a level of nothingness. Just peace, life slowing down.

Since the Cup things have changed a bit. There is still that lovely feeling of serenity, but now as she rides she replays the race over in her mind.

Everything Maddie does revolves around Prince Of Penzance. He is the main man in her life. This is not a chore. Maddie believes in doing what makes you happy, and this horse makes her happy. She jokes that her wedding day will be a bit of a disappointment compared to the joy he has given her.

Sometimes someone will say that of course she loves a Melbourne Cup winner. But the bond between horse and rider was well and truly set in stone long before then.

Maddie did not grow up in a horsey household. In fact, her parents held no interest in the equine whatsoever. But she cannot remember a time when she did not love horses. She grew up wanting a pony.

As soon as she could she got a job at a local trail riding establishment, and her ambition of owning a horse was fulfilled when she was thirteen — an ex-polo thoroughbred cross by the name of Skye.

While still at school Maddie worked at the local stables of Matthew Williams, afternoons and weekends. Some time with Darren Weir and upon turning eighteen, she moved to Melbourne to work for David Hayes. And then it was back home as a foreman at Darren Weir's Warrnambool stables.

In early 2015, she enjoyed a stint in Ireland working for champion National Hunt trainer Willie Mullins, an amazing experience, she said, 'a massive learning curve'.

It was there that she would ride the talented galloper Max Dynamite, who had been successfully mixing flat and jumps racing.

A Group Three win in the Lonsdale Cup at York in August 2015 secured him a run in the Melbourne Cup, so come the spring Maddie would get to see him again.

On Melbourne Cup Day, her concentration centred on one horse. She was up at 3am, having hardly slept. Being an organised person she had everything ready to go.

Her first job for the morning was to shampoo her charge, to check him over and make sure all was okay. Then it was to the beach for Prince Of Penzance's last bit of work, an easy ride off the pony at Lady Bay.

Maddie rode with friends to Flemington, the excitement mounting. In the float behind them Prince Of Penzance stood calmly and quietly, though once on course he was impatient to get out and get on with things.

At the track it was Maddie's job to keep Prince Of Penzance relaxed and happy. That proved an easy task, the horse as content as he had ever been on a race day.

It was one of the first things Michelle Payne noticed, just how composed this amazing horse was on a furiously busy, crowded and noisy day.

Maddie and Prince Of Penzance did a fair bit of walking, around and around the rose-lined Flemington birdcage. Lots of people came to see him and his Melbourne Cup rivals, many a photo taken by the racing paparazzi.

Maddie's nerves grew as the race approached. She knew the horse could not be in any better order. Darren Weir, she says, 'knows just how to time them right to the minute'.

Maddie watched the Melbourne Cup from the mounting yard. She was separated from her mates, including her best (human) friend, fellow strapper Sarah Woodhouse.

From the time the gates opened she held her breath. When Prince Of Penzance made his winning run she didn't make a sound.

'When he got out into the clear and pinned his ears back I knew he had it. Michelle had given him a perfect ride and I knew how fit he was, I knew he wasn't going to stop.'

There is not a more exciting moment in horse racing, but Maddie did not cheer or scream. She just stood there trembling as madness ensued around her. She remembers Sarah barging through security to get to her, hugging her and crying, telling her how proud she was of her.

And then there was Stevie Payne, who was so overcome with emotion that he grabbed Maddie, hugging her tightly, unable to let go.

Through all the madness Maddie's first concern was for Prince Of Penzance. Returning from races in the past he could be quite pushy and she already had a feeling he'd pulled up well, so far after the line had he galloped on.

He was so much on his toes upon his return that Maddie had to really focus on making sure that he and everyone around him was kept safe.

'He is not a mean horse, but if someone was to stand in front of him he'd just walk through them,' she laughed.

As soon as the photos were taken of Prince Of Penzance resplendent in his shiny red rug, Maddie took him back to his stall. He had a wash, a drink, and within no time was in recovery mode.

'I thought he'd be tired enough to give me a bit of a break but he wasn't!' Maddie said. 'I have worked with so many great horses with Darren, but I'd never come across ones as tough as this one.'

Melbourne Cup Day was a long one for Maddie. After driving all the way back to Warrnambool and tucking in her boy for the night she was driven by friends to Ballarat for the stable celebrations.

And she was back aboard Prince Of Penzance the next morning, unable to believe what great shape he was in; he was bouncing. 'Never before had I even come close to falling off him but I did that morning! He was so full of himself.'

The following week was a hectic one, lots of celebrations with friends and family. Work was still busy so not much sleep was had, but it became of secondary importance, Maddie keen to embrace the experience.

An invitation from Michelle Payne to enjoy a post-spring carnival holiday in Bali was one that Maddie was first hesitant about, not knowing any of Michelle's friends.

'But she was adamant that I'd fit right in. So I went for a week, in which we spent relaxing and reminiscing. It was a great time to reflect and rest.'

Maddie has continued to work hard since, maintaining her special connection with her special horse. And no matter what happens now, Prince Of Penzance's 2015 Melbourne Cup victory will always be held dear. 'Every time I think of the race or see a photo of it I get goosebumps, and that is a feeling that will never go away.'

Hoofnote: When asked to allow Stevie Payne to be a major part of Melbourne Cup Day, Maddie did not hesitate. She was, said the stable's Michael Leonard, 'extremely gracious'.

'There is absolutely no ego to her, and when it was her chance to be the centre of attention she stepped aside. She is an extremely impressive young lady.'

Chapter Twenty-Three

PETER ELLIS

'A perfect union.'

That is how Peter Ellis describes his professional relationship with Darren Weir, one which began rather informally at a Ballarat race meeting in September 2012.

Darren had seen Peter around, but knew him only enough to nod and say a quick g'day to.

Peter, whose passion for horse racing has seen him regularly spending his weekends at the track for forty-five years — even racing when he travels — of course knew who Darren was.

At that stage working as a form analyst for RadioTAB and also contributing to *The Age*'s form guide, Peter had earned a reputation as a great judge of racing form.

Building his own database over decades — twenty-five years ago, with the help of his brother-in-law converting it to a computer program — Peter has intricate knowledge of how tracks race in different conditions, which horses will be most suited on which day, and how they are best ridden.

Every regular racegoer has seen Peter out on the track, early and throughout the day as patterns change. For the first few races leaders may be suited, but as that part of the turf suffers from wear and tear it may be better later to be out wider.

There are no set rules and things change quickly. It takes a lot of research and an astute mind to take it all in, to process the information and use it to advantage.

Darren Weir knew that racing tactics were not his strong point. So when he happened to walk past Peter at Ballarat that day he thought there'd be no harm in asking for some advice.

Coming off a Mildura Cup win was the stable's talented and consistent galloper, Lord Of Brazil. He was a favoured runner in that day's feature event, the Gold Nugget Stakes, and Darren was wondering if he could be ridden a little differently to usual.

A horse who normally settled midfield, finishing off strongly, Lord Of Brazil had drawn wide, but Weir was keen to see him closer to the pace. However, he didn't know if others would be working forward as well.

Which is where Peter and his speed maps — predictions of how races will be run and won — came in. He asked Peter his opinion, and after careful study of the race it was offered.

Yes, Peter said, Lord Of Brazil could be up there and win.

And so Darren instructed jockey Luke Currie to ride the horse forward. He sat outside the leader and on the line had a length on his nearest rival … an easy winner.

Was it a fluke? Darren and Peter locked heads for another race later in the day … another winner.

For six or so months after that Peter advised Darren on a casual basis. And then it became a permanent arrangement. Since which time Darren's annual figures have improved … and improved again.

'Peter has been a massive help,' Darren said. 'He takes the pressure off me regarding tactics, and it is great to have access to such great knowledge.'

Peter attends every metropolitan meeting where the Weir stable has runners. On major days he heads interstate, such as the day Howard Be Thy Name won the South Australian Derby at Morphettville.

Darren had runners elsewhere and Peter was the stable representative on track. It was something he regarded as an honour, stoked by the faith Darren had in him.

At Flemington in February 2016, the Weir trained Palentino was first past the post in the Colin Hayes Stakes, only to lose the race on protest.

Darren shook his head — he had never had much luck in protest hearings. Maybe Peter could do better. And so the stewards were approached and permission was granted for him to be the stable's representative at future hearings.

And it so happened that the same horse was protested against just two weeks later. He had won a major race, the Australian Guineas, and there was great media interest in the outcome.

Not one for the spotlight, Peter nevertheless handled it all with his usual laidback aplomb, arguing the case intelligently and thoughtfully … and the protest was dismissed.

Describing Darren as 'very easy to work with', Peter is one of the lucky ones to earn a living doing something he loves.

'This has been my hobby and my profession since I was a teenager,' he said.

Always fascinated by the idea that a race result could not be conclusively predicted, that each Saturday morning nobody knew which horses would emerge victorious, Peter applied his mathematical skills to putting the odds in his favour.

He has learned how to be forgiving of runs, how not to underestimate or overestimate certain form. Which tracks suit which horses, which don't.

It has never been, he says, purely about the punt. It is more the challenge and about racing itself, an involvement in an exciting sport with great people.

And it has been about history, Peter excited seeing a horse like High Chaparral win an Epsom Derby in 2002, and seven years later being on course at Moonee Valley to see his brilliant son So You

Think win the first of his two W. S. Cox Plates.

He has seen many great horses, Kingston Town a local favourite while overseas Sea The Stars and Zenyatta, darling of the American turf, impressed.

When starting to work for Darren Weir, Peter had three aims.

To win a Group One, which was soon achieved with the 2013 Robert Sangster Stakes winner Platelet.

To win a Group One race in Victoria, something at that stage Darren Weir had not achieved. He did so with Trust In A Gust in September 2014.

And for Darren to win the trainers premiership.

It was tick, tick, tick for Peter, but Darren had always had his eye on something even bigger. His dream was to win the Melbourne Cup.

Much of Peter's knowledge is shared by other racing analysts, but he has the advantage of having travelled with his profession. He has studied form around the world and has walked tracks in England, Japan, South Africa, France, Ireland, America, New Zealand, Hong Kong, Dubai, Germany and Singapore.

This is something that gives him a distinct advantage when studying the form for Australia's most internationalised race, the Melbourne Cup. A race he says you can increase your chances of winning 300–400 percent by careful study.

Collating his own data on forty runnings of the race, Peter knows 'what sort of horse is required'.

Peter walked the Flemington track five times on Melbourne Cup Day 2015. A pivotal moment came when he just happened to be out there at the same time as a jockey.

Michelle Payne.

In his hand at the time he had a printout. Each of Darren's regular riders — Michelle, Brad Rawiller, Harry Coffey, John Allen and Dean Yendall — receive them.

While other jockeys often don't hear their instructions until they are in the mounting yard close to the race, Darren's have them in print, in hand some time before the race. Time to study, time to think.

With Michelle on the track at the same time as Peter there was an opportunity to discuss the race together. Follow Criterion and Max Dynamite, he said, put the horse to sleep behind them and get off the fence at the 600 metres — there could be interference shortly afterwards.

In the straight Peter walked out to where he thought would be the best place to be. Out a few metres from the fence, no more than eight. From there, he said, see how many horses you can pass.

That was Plan A and there was no Plan B. So from there it was up to Michelle, Prince Of Penzance and, says Peter, 'a bit of divine intervention'.

Prince Of Penzance was, of course, a little slowly away, which is where Michelle's skills kicked in. She didn't panic as she urged him into the planned position, the moment Peter (who noted that Darren does not 'usually like them booted up after a slow start') describes as 'the winning move'.

'Nobody in the world could've ridden him better that day,' Peter said.

It was a privilege, Peter says, to be involved in a Melbourne Cup victory. All the more so in such a special one, one he describes as 'an absolute fairytale'.

Over the course of Prince Of Penzance's career Peter has befriended the horse's owners, delighted that such a good horse is owned by a large group.

A group of people who certainly appreciate Peter's efforts and who were keen to have him celebrate with them at The Emerald on Cup Night. But, ever vigilant and dedicated, he was back at home preparing for Oaks Day. The racing show must go on!

Part Four

THE OWNERS

'We have experienced something amazing together.'

PRINCE OF PENZANCE, MELBOURNE CUP WINNER. Portrait by Adam Michael Rumsby, from a photo by Lisa Grimm

top: PENTIRE, sire of Prince Of Penzance, June 2016. Photo courtesy of Rich Hill Stud

bottom: DARREN WEIR WITH AUSTY COFFEY. Darren Weir at his first job in Birchup, Victoria. Photo courtesy of Jack Coffey

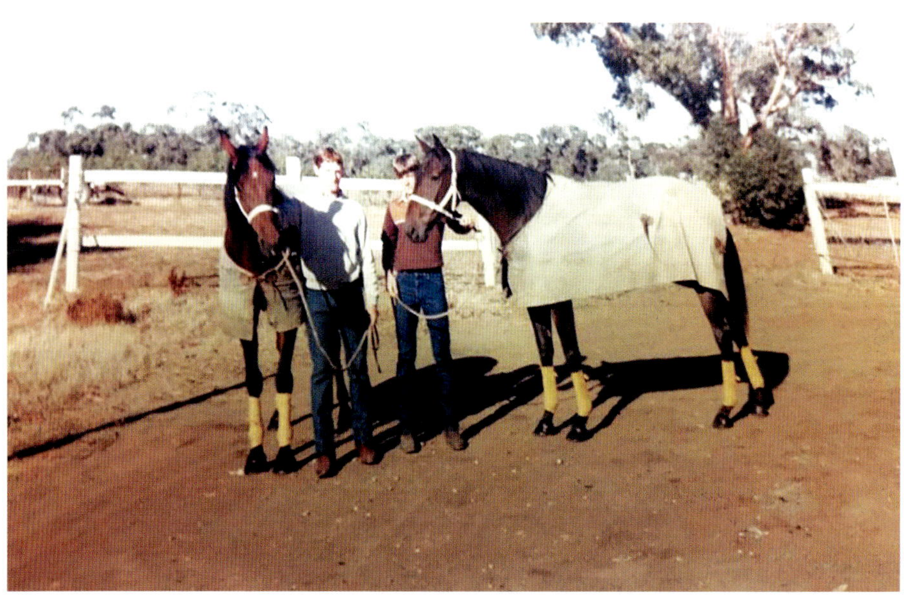

MADDIE RAYMOND with Prince Of Penzance at Warrnambool. Photo by Sharon Chapman

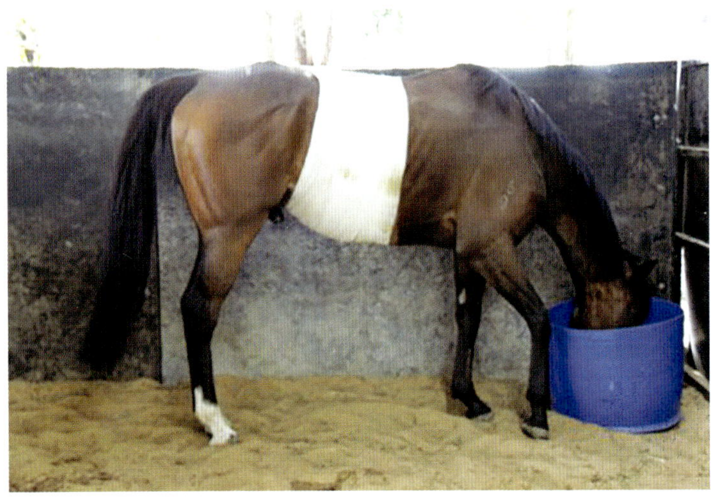

top: PRINCE OF PENZANCE PLAYS SECOND STRING TO BLACK CAVIAR. Caulfield, 20 April 2013. Photo by Andrew Wilson

bottom: PRINCE OF PENZANCE RECOVERS FROM COLIC OPERATION. February 2015. Photo by Pam Wilson

top: THE BOYS AT WORK. Peter Ellis and Darren Weir discuss tactics. Photo by Kristen Manning

bottom: BARRIER ONE! Stevie Payne draws the winning barrier. Photo by Sharon Chapman

top: THE MELBOURNE CUP PARADE. Michelle Payne, Emily Lonsdale and Jessica McGregor. Photo by Darren Lonsdale

middle: MEN IN HATS. The syndicate meet up before the running of the 2015 Melbourne Cup. Photo courtesy of Men In Hats

bottom: THE CUP ARRIVES. VRC Chairman Michael Burn. Photo by Sharon Chapman

top: MICHELLE PAYNE returns from pre-race jockey presentation next to Gérald Mossé, rider of Red Cadeaux. Photo by Sharon Chapman

bottom: AT THE GATES. Photo by Sarah Ebbett

M. Payne
PRINCE OF PENZANCE

M.J.Payne
PRINCE OF PENZANC

opposite top: OUT OF THE STRAIGHT. The Melbourne Cup field makes the first turn, Prince Of Penzance is midfield on the rails. Photo by Sharon Chapman

opposite middle: VICTORY IN SIGHT. Michelle Payne roars at Prince Of Penzance. Photo by Sarah Ebbett

opposite bottom: WINNER. Prince Of Penzance wins an unforgettable Melbourne Cup. Photo by Sharon Chapman

top: THE WINNING TEAM RETURNS. Maddie, Michelle and Stevie. Photo by Sarah Ebbett

bottom: SISTER AND BROTHER CELEBRATE. Michelle and Stevie. Photo by Sarah Ebbett

top: THE HERO RETURNS. Prince Of Penzance's owners are all smiles as he returns to scale. Photo by Peter Morganti

middle: HAPPY OWNERS. (L–R) Bruce Dalton, David Wilson and Sandy Dalton. Photo by Sarah Ebbett

bottom: MICHELLE CONGRATULATES OWNERS. John Richards and Darren Lonsdale. Photo by Sharon Chapman

top: TEARFUL JOY. Darren Weir embraced by his daughters Bonnie and Taige. Photo by Peter Morganti

left: DARREN AND MICHELLE. Photo by Peter Morganti

right: WE'VE WON THE CUP! Sandy McGregor holds the Cup aloft. Photo by Sarah Ebbett

top: HAPPY FAMILY. Owner Andrew Broadford with wife Kim, and daughters (L–R) Alice, Molly and Sapphire. Photo by Sharon Chapman

bottom: HAPPY COUPLE. Owner Greg Williams and fiancée Alex Patrick. Photo by Sharon Chapman

left: WINNERS ROOM CELEBRATIONS. (L–R) Neil Laws, David Wilson, Stephen Wilson, Jeremy Rogers, Ken Laws, Michael Wilson, Pam Wilson and Andrew Wilson. Photo by Dave Pullen

right: FATHER AND DAUGHTERS. Arthur Rickard celebrates with his daughters Jenny Monks and Susan Cahill. Photo by Rod Cahill

bottom: AT THE EMERALD. Brothers Bruce, Joe and Jonathon Dalton with Michelle Payne. Photo courtesy of Bruce Dalton

MELBOURNE CUP WINNING BREEDERS. Presentation of the Breeders Melbourne Cup to John Thompson at Ellerslie, January 2016. (L–R) Alan Galbraith QC, William, Emma, Colleen and John Thompson, and Michelle Payne. Photo courtesy of Rich Hill Stud

top: DARREN WEIR'S HOME TOWN. Photo by Bobby Borlase

bottom: BERRIWILLOCK'S TRIBUTE. Bobby Borlase and the wall at the Golden Crown. Photo by Vin Lowe

top: THE CUP VISITS THE BEACH. Maddie, Prince Of Penzance, the Cup and owners (L–R) Neil and Keith Laws, Pam and David Wilson. Photo courtesy of Wilawl Go Racing

bottom: RED CADEAUX shares a tender moment with Robin Trevor-Jones before his final race. Photo by Sharon Chapman

Chapter Twenty-Four

JOHN RICHARDS

JOHN Richards has been racing horses for a few decades now and he is an old hand at it. He knows how long it takes, the ups and the downs, the odds against finding the pot of equine gold.

It's a lengthy process, he knows ... 'all you ever do with horses is wait', he jokes. But it is one he enjoys. That initial hope that your horse will make it to the races, that it may win a maiden.

And when it does show promise, the excitement of dreaming of a city-class horse. And maybe even better.

He has been through all of this before. He has raced some talented horses, the likes of Lake Sententia, Royal Bender, Ava's Delight and Scarlet Billows putting winning photos on his walls.

He started off small with a couple of horses, not an auspicious start with one of those winning one lowly race, the other dying under mysterious circumstances.

Then one day he met Darren Weir, and as that trainer's stable grew so did John's.

With experience on his side John has a pretty good idea of whether or not a horse has what it takes. It is not impossible to predict, as a horse rises through the grades, whether or not it is going to get to a high level.

But there is one race that is more of a dream than a goal.

It is, of course, the Melbourne Cup. Just getting a horse to the race is an amazing thrill for the owner. And it is an achievement for that horse, to make it to the elite field.

Once your horse is there you know he is a talented stayer.

But it is not, says John, 'until he crosses the line in front that you know you have got a Melbourne Cup horse'.

Backtrack a few years to when John was first offered a share in Prince Of Penzance. He owns quite a few horses and has a criteria with breeding the focus.

'Pedigree is number one,' he said.

And Prince Of Penzance certainly had the breeding. He was by Pentire, a stallion John had always respected — 'He is a wonderful stallion, I love him … who doesn't?'

And his dam was by the mighty Mr Prospector, also advantageous.

Astute judge John Foote had selected this particular Pentire and John valued his opinion. 'That ticked another box,' he said.

And considering his pedigree, John laughed, 'I thought he was a bloody cheap horse!'

And he was not wrong, Prince Of Penzance proving to be the best investment of the horse kind that John has made.

It is not money, though, that drives John to race horses. He knows, like any owner, that seldom is a profit made. It is more the thrill of competition, the friendships made along the way, the love of the horse.

And John really loves Prince Of Penzance. He has been there for most of his runs, visiting him at the stables in between, spending long hours in the car to watch him trial at out-of-the-way tracks.

He went to Flemington on Melbourne Cup Day, confident that his horse would run well, regarding the odds on offer almost an insult.

'But odds feed off themselves,' he said. 'A punter sees 50–1 and thinks that horse has no hope, so the price just gets bigger and bigger.'

John remembers being at Cranbourne races the week before the Melbourne Cup, noticing on his phone that Prince Of Penzance was 60–1. Those odds were just too tempting, so he had a bet.

Next time he checked he was 80–1, so he had another. And then he was 100–1. A friend showed him his Betfair account — only a small bet was on offer but someone was willing to give 280–1 odds that Prince Of Penzance would win.

The market may have underestimated Prince Of Penzance but John, who describes his horse as 'so tough', did not.

'He is an energetic horse, one who wants to get on with things. When he sees a gap in a race he takes it. Most horses have to be pushed through them, but not him.

Watching the Melbourne Cup from the owners seating in the old members grandstand, John was confident a fair way out. As the race unfolded I knew it was only a matter of time before he challenged.'

Like his co-owners, John found the winning moments surreal. He wanted to be in the mounting yard as quickly as possible but faced a sea of security. Once there he stood watching his horse as friends offered their congratulations. His pose was one of a man in a fair amount of shock!

John's Melbourne Cup story begins with his family. He was born and raised in St Arnaud, 120 kilometres south of Darren Weir's home town Berriwillock.

His uncle was the local SP (starting price) bookmaker, the hairdresser the shop front, the serious business of punting taking place out the back.

Until the introduction of the TAB in 1961, the only legal way to have a bet was on course. And so SP bookmakers flourished across the country, becoming part of Australian folklore.

Saturdays with his uncle were looked forward to by John, who said the bookmakers headquarters 'always seemed like such a happy place, full of people having fun'.

It left an impression on John, who was twenty-seven when he

purchased his first two horses, and he has 'had at least one horse ever since'.

Supporting Darren Weir from early days, John remembers that even when inexperienced there was something about him. 'He was so focused. But easy to get on with, having a horse with him was … and is … fun.'

The Melbourne Cup was not the first milestone John and Darren have enjoyed together. Darren's first Melbourne city winner Rather Yallah (Moonee Valley, November 2000) was bred and raced by John.

And John's gold and green colours were also worn by Rather Heroic, who at Cranbourne on 23 January 2015 — ridden by Michelle Payne — was Darren's 2000th winner.

He also bred and raced the city winner Palentine Hill, dam of Darren's 2016 Group One Australian Guineas winner Palentino.

And he races Scarlet Billows, the second leg of the Weir stable's Melbourne Cup Day double. Just 2 1/4 hours after the big race John was again in the winner's circle.

But he was not surprised to be there, having had a strong feeling in the lead up that Scarlet Billows would win that race, the Group Three Hong Kong Jockey Club Stakes.

'I was just really confident. I thought Prince Of Penzance would be competitive, but I really thought Scarlet Billows would win.'

John, who enjoyed the day with his family present, remembers thinking to himself as he headed to the committee room after the final race, *I've not had a bad day!*

A day that kicked on, John heading first to The Emerald and then to Ballarat, noting that Darren was still going strong when he left at 2am.

A week after Prince Of Penzance's Melbourne Cup victory, John took the trophy home to Ballarat. Staff at Goldacres, his highly successful company, one that produces spraying equipment for farms across the country, were delighted to see it.

'Everyone was pretty excited, it really boosted morale,' he said, noting that people are used to such amazing things happening to people they don't know.

Winning the Melbourne Cup, he says, has created a bond between him and his fellow owners of Prince Of Penzance — 'We have experienced something amazing together.'

Everywhere John goes the Melbourne Cup is mentioned. When he takes a trip home to St Arnaud where Goldacres grew from a business started by his father, he is congratulated.

Attending a local football match the winter after the race, he was invited to speak about the Melbourne Cup and was gratified by the response — 'People hung on my every word.'

Chapter Twenty-Five

SANDY McGREGOR

SANDY McGregor is not joking when he says he doesn't take any notice of sprinting races.

'I don't even bother to turn on the television to watch unless the race is 2000 metres or over,' he says. 'And I know more about jumps racing in the United Kingdom than I do about the local sprinters.'

Sandy's passion is, and always has been, the stayer.

'Staying racing is,' he says, 'such a spectacular and endearing part of racing.'

And while the Australian thoroughbred breeding industry focuses on speed, our richest, most famous, most challenging race is contested every November at Flemington over 3200 metres.

It was the race Sandy had always wanted to win, an aim he shared with Darren Weir. A dream come true on Tuesday, 3 November 2015.

While his fellow owners described the moment Prince Of Penzance crossed the line to win the Melbourne Cup in understandably emotive terms, Sandy said his overriding feeling was one of 'relief'.

For the Melbourne Cup is a race he has long studied, long thought about. He has given careful consideration to which sort of horses win it and has bought horses who fit the criteria.

These are horses such as Signoff, the tough and classy stayer he races with Gerry Ryan. Purchased on his behalf by John Foote at a yearling sale at Newmarket, England, in October 2011, the Darren Weir trained gelding has won eight of his eighteen starts.

Fourth as equal third favourite in the 2014 Melbourne Cup won by the German bred Protectionist, Signoff has had his issues. But he won a 2600-metre Group Three event in Adelaide in March, and is on track for another crack at the big one. Which means, if all goes to plan, Sandy may be cheering on two horses at Flemington in November 2016.

Like everyone else involved with Prince Of Penzance, he is still celebrating the 2015 race, a race he was not all that surprised to win.

'It sounds stupid, but I had always thought that I would one day win the Melbourne Cup,' he said.

Especially as he knew he was in the right stable, always confident in Darren Weir's ability to get the best out of a promising staying horse.

'Prince Of Penzance was his first Melbourne Cup winner, but I don't think he will be his last.'

Sandy's association with Darren Weir goes well back.

Raised at Callawadda, not too far from where Darren kicked off his training career at Stawell, Sandy was born into a racing family — his father Stuart was a long-serving president of the Stawell Racing Club.

Stuart and Judith McGregor were early Darren Weir supporters, their horse Brechan Bay winning ten races all around Victoria. It was only natural that their son would follow in their racing footsteps.

In tune with his appreciation of stayers is Sandy's love of jumpers. He has raced two of the best in recent times, the half-brothers Black And Bent and Some Are Bent who between them won thirty-five races, including three Grand National Hurdles and a host of other features.

In May 2016, appointed Chairman of the Australian Jumping Racing Association, Sandy notes that staying racing and jumps racing go hand in hand; they are 'pie and sauce'.

It frustrates him that staying racing does not have greater respect in a country where the Melbourne Cup reigns. Though, as one of the minority who specifically target distance races, it has put the odds in his favour.

And it is not just a matter of finding the right horses but, of course, the right trainer. Bart Cummings was one, he says, Darren Weir another. There are some who will never win a Melbourne Cup. They don't have the patience, the skills, the facilities.

Darren Weir has all three.

The way his stables are set up at Ballarat and Warrnambool, says Sandy, play a big part in his success with staying horses. They can run free and straight, up hills and sand dunes, through waves.

Horses trained in the city are restricted to hard, tight turning tracks that are more often than not placed in the centre of race courses. That means more pressure on their joints, their muscles.

Over his years of watching the Melbourne Cup emerge as an international contest, Sandy has never lost faith that locally bred and trained horses can still win the big race, even when doomsayers were predicting that the race would be forever at the mercy of the Europeans and the Japanese.

And so he is not into buying tried horses in an attempt to win the Melbourne Cup. He prefers to start from scratch, and even his import Signoff was purchased as a yearling.

'The home ground advantage has to be massive,' he says, 'it has got to be lengths.'

And Sandy is a patient owner. A horse who turned seven in August 2016, Signoff has raced just eighteen times. Prince Of Penzance, the same age, won the Melbourne Cup at his twenty-fourth start.

'He always had untapped ability,' he said of Prince Of Penzance, adding that it was 'the genius of D. K. Weir to get him to produce the run on the day that counted'.

Chapter Twenty-Six

THE DALTONS

EACH year the iconic Melbourne Cup trophy embarks on an Australia-wide tour, since 2003 the solid gold Loving Cup (a design in place since 1919, first handed to the connections of Artilleryman) heading far and wide.

It visits schools, nursing homes, small outback communities and race meetings. It is embraced by all who come into contact with it. It has a mystique, an aura.

Despite growing up at Bundaberg, some 1879 kilometres away from Flemington, Bruce Dalton always knew that the Melbourne Cup was something special.

'The whole time going through school we stopped for the Melbourne Cup. Everyone had sweeps, it was a big thing even when we were too young to know what it was all about.'

Bruce certainly knew how special the race was when he won it, when he held it. His own Melbourne Cup, shared with twenty-three other owners, including his fellow members of Dalton Racing, his brothers Joe and Jonathon.

But it was not until he saw the pleasure that it brought to others that he truly realised just what a special piece of Australiana the Melbourne Cup trophy is.

The Dalton family had no big plans when it was their turn

to take care of the Melbourne Cup. It was enough just to have it and admire it. They did not seek attention; they did not contact any media.

But when a friend of a colleague asked if he could bring it to a local primary school, Bruce thought that was a great idea.

And so it began. The 2015 Melbourne Cup's second tour was one that took in twenty-five or so schools, retirement villages, hospitals and four northern and central Queensland race meetings.

Everywhere it went it elicited joy.

Australia's twenty-fourth biggest town, Bundaberg, had never before played host to a Melbourne Cup, and Bruce was overwhelmed by the response.

'The phone just kept ringing and I figured because I was self-employed I had the time. I could take it to whoever wanted it. We wanted as many people as possible to see it.'

Often providing gloves for the handling, Bruce was, however, not at all precious about the trophy. 'It may have got a few dings along the way but it is solid gold so you can't break it. So long as everyone respects it, which they did, happy days.'

Several moments stand out in Bruce's memory, such as a Grade 6 girl welling up in tears as she held it … 'That made me think, *Wow what have we got here?!*'

Grade 3 students, who had dressed up in race wear at Thabeban State School, cheered as the Cup was presented at assembly. Parents also turned up, unwilling to miss out on such an opportunity, and a Melbourne Cup parade was held, with local news stations in attendance.

The Cup went to a blood bank in order to promote the need for increased donations, and it brought smiles to the faces of patients at Bundaberg Hospital.

At a nursing home a World War II veteran sat in his barren room. He was blind so he could not see the Cup, but he could hold it. And as he did he recalled the day he and a mate, on leave from the navy, headed to Flemington with a hot tip, winning a hundred pounds, a huge amount at the time. As he told the story, memories of his youth returned and he cried.

Racegoers at Bundaberg, Gladstone, Rockhampton and Mackay also had the chance to access the Cup, though one lady at the latter's race meeting was a little confused, asking Bruce, 'Is that the trophy for the Fashions On The Field winner?'

But the majority of people knew exactly what it was, such as a couple of racehorse owners who tipped Bruce their horse one day, asking if they could include the trophy in their presentation.

And so there they were, proud owners of the last winner at Gladstone one day, holding their horse in one hand, the Melbourne Cup in the other.

Bruce enjoyed taking the Cup to his (and his father's and grandfather's) old school Nudgee College, where students told the local press that 'it's cool, really awesome, you don't get to see a Melbourne Cup every day'.

The Victoria Racing Club's Joe McGrath was not surprised to hear how well the Melbourne Cup was received. He has been travelling around Australia with it for over a decade and is still astounded by the reaction.

'The popularity of the Emirates Melbourne Cup never ceases to amaze those connected with the Victoria Racing Club, what it means to people across Australia and New Zealand. As we have taken it on the road to over 333 communities since 2003 we have come to appreciate very quickly that it is very much part of the Australian cultural identity.

'I set off thinking it was a sporting icon, but it's more than that, it is a cultural icon. It has been a constant in the development of the nation, it has been there through good times and bad times, through gold rushes, through wars and the Great Depression. It draws an emotional response from the youngest to the oldest, and is a symbol of what Australians are all about.

'As the 2015 Emirates Melbourne Cup has come to prove, dreams can come true and 100–1 chances can still win the race. Australians love that aspect. Coupled with the fact that we had the first female winning rider of the Cup, it was truly inspirational.'

In June 2016, travelling back to Melbourne to hand the Melbourne Cup over to another set of Prince Of Penzance's happy owners, Bruce and Jonathon enjoyed a day out at Moonee Valley in a dining box named after the most famous Cup winner of all — the legendary Phar Lap.

And once again the Cup created a stir, passed from table to table, the reaction of everybody present being sheer delight. Members of the Melbourne Rebels rugby union team posed for photos, visitors from interstate could not believe their luck being able to hold a Melbourne Cup.

Especially a Melbourne Cup whose story has already been written, one belonging to a particular horse. In years to come they will be telling the tale of the day they held Prince Of Penzance's Cup.

And that gives Bruce a special thrill, especially as, on the day and in the weeks afterwards, much of the Cup publicity understandably had its focus on Michelle Payne.

'In ten years' time I think it will be a trivial pursuit question,' he joked. 'Which horse did Michelle Payne win the Melbourne Cup on?'

Always 'mad keen punters', the Dalton brothers decided only a few years ago that it would be fun to have a horse together. Joe had raced a few before, but Bruce and Jonathon were novices. They started with a leased share but with no success. 'We are pretty sure that horse had only three legs,' Jonathon laughed.

Stayers had always appealed to them and so Joe set about doing some research. When he noticed that John Foote had secured a well-related son of Pentire for just $50,000 at the Karaka sales he was soon on the phone.

'John said he thought he'd got the horse for half his value,' Joe recalled. 'He was a late foal, a bit on the small side and early in the sale, so he sold for a lot less than he probably should have.'

Joe knew a bargain when he saw it and was happy with their new horse, especially when Darren Weir told the owners that the horse would not be racing as a two-year-old … they were in for the long haul and were content to be patient.

It was patience that paid dividends on Melbourne Cup Day 2015. The three brothers were all on course at Flemington, a special day as Joe had been fighting serious illness for months, given time off chemotherapy to make it south.

They watched the race from the owners seats behind the mounting yard, a fair way from the finishing line. But it ended up being just the right place to be, with Prince Of Penzance beginning his memorable winning run just in front of them.

Looking around, the Daltons found themselves surrounded by wealthy English and Japanese owners, all stern and aristocratic.

'And here we were, the blokes from northern Queensland,' Bruce laughed.

He could not help but wonder at the time, 'What are we doing here?' For days he had read negative comments about his horse in the press, things like 'this horse will need a jet-pack attached to his back to win this' or 'if you get this horse in the sweep palm him off to the office drunk'.

But then he thought, there are only twenty-four horses here. And their boy was one of them. He had earned his place.

It was a long Cup Day for Joe, Bruce and Jonathon. They were up very early, out to Flemington in plenty of time, enjoying the great view afforded by reserved seats in the Hill Stand.

For the first part of the day they were like any other racegoers, standing in long queues for a drink and a bet. But then they got to do something only a select few each year get to enjoy, to watch their own horse run in the Melbourne Cup.

And what an experience that was. At the 400 metres Joe calmly said to his brothers, 'We are a top ten chance.'

At the 200 metres Jonathon more excitedly said, 'Top five!'

And at the 100 metres Joe roared, 'We are going to win the Melbourne Cup!'

There may have been a swear word or two in there somewhere as well — such raw emotions are not always politely expressed!

It was, said Bruce, a surreal experience. 'It is 155 years of history, to win it was staggering.'

So fast did the celebrations fly by that Bruce forgot to eat, his celebratory dinner a lukewarm pie late that night. Jonathon looked at his watch just before the race and the next time he checked it was 1am.

A couple of hours after the race, Racing Victoria's automated email to owners appeared: the result of the race. Bruce had seen those sorts of emails many times, but he just stared at this one. It was the Melbourne Cup!

In the committee room after the race, an owner of the fourth-placed UK raider Trip To Paris, Andy Gemmell, was one of the first to congratulate them. There was no disappointment in his demeanour, he was just keen to say well done to those who had won, having his photo taken with them and saying he'd be back next year.

At the end of the day Joe, Bruce and Jonathon joined a long taxi queue. When they eventually hailed a maxi cab they found themselves in with a couple of blokes who found it hard to believe who was sharing their ride.

'Shouldn't you be heading home in a helicopter?' they said.

At The Emerald that night the celebrations were long and loud. The Daltons happened to be in the public bar when Darren Weir wandered in with the trophy … 'The place went wild.'

Later on the brothers stood outside on the footpath with Michelle, a couple of beers and the Cup. It's a memory that will stick with them forever. An extra-special memory because in July 2016, Joe passed away.

Chapter Twenty-Seven

MEN IN HATS

'WE all knew that it was a once-in-a-lifetime experience and we were just going to make the most of the day.'

No real expectations from the group of six friends that make up the Men In Hats Syndicate, part-owners of Prince Of Penzance.

'We were all happy with the idea of a top ten finish,' said syndicate manager Sam Brown, who now laughs at his initial belief that he had handled Cup Day with anxiety-free aplomb.

It was not until he watched the video shot in the mounting yard pre-race that he saw the stress on his face, a look that only intensified once the field was off and running.

For Prince Of Penzance was positioned perfectly, just where Michelle Payne had hoped to be. Soon he had settled into a lovely rhythm. And the better he travelled, the tenser experience it became for those watching from the mounting yard, which is where the Men In Hats group had congregated.

Shifting from foot to foot, a bit of nail biting, the occasional grimacing, some hand rubbing as they watched the action unfold on the big screen, chatting to each other about their horse's progress.

At the top of the straight: 'She's got him out.' With 420 metres to go: 'Go Pop!', 'C'mon Pop!', some screaming, 'Go, go, go, go!'

And he hits the lead. What did his owners feel at that amazing moment? For Greg Williams it was disbelief. For Sam, well he was in shock … standing in silence for the final stages of the race, which Mike Botting described as 'the best fifty metres of watching any racehorse ever!'

And then, as Greg Miles declared, 'history at Flemington' — mayhem, shock turning into elation. Star jumps, fist pumps, hugs, tears, back slapping, a lot of yelling, everyone's mobile phones buzzing in pockets as hundreds of messages poured in.

Adrian Brown saying over and over, 'Did that just happen, did that happen?' Another voice, that of fellow owner Darren Lonsdale, roaring, 'A dream, a dream.' Scott Jenke desperately scanning the ground for his glasses lost in the commotion. Tim Ashford and Greg Williams hugging so hard that the latter is injured — he is bleeding from the mouth but he doesn't care.

And Sam falls to his knees. For him it was a moment of joy tinged with grief. For in his pocket was a memorial card, to his son Edward who just four months previously had not survived a tragically difficult birth. Sam and his wife Connie's world collapsed and it was hard to see the light at the end of the tunnel. But Prince Of Penzance provided a glimmer, a horse who showed the couple that 'good things can still happen'.

'My wife and I are sure that Prince winning the Cup was a miracle, a sign above from Edward. The day before I had thought about how I would acknowledge him if the craziest thing happened, and we won. I put the memorial card photo in my pocket for good luck and once I had got off my knees I leapt up and kissed the sky as a tribute to Edward. When I finally caught up with Connie she was in tears, asking, "Did you think about Edward?" I reached into my pocket and showed her the card. For me that was the most special moment of the whole day, and it gives me some positive thoughts about my lost boy. I will always associate the Melbourne Cup with his memory.'

The post-race mounting yard revelling continued as there was plenty of time, with the ever-enthusiastic Prince Of Penzance taking so long to pull up that Michelle's horseback interview was conducted way over the other side of the track. Other jockeys later told her that they had wanted to catch up with her to offer their congratulations but they couldn't get anywhere near her strong galloping horse!

The winners room was the first of many parties for the Men In Hats group. The Emerald, the casino … and lots of other places, from backyards to pubs and restaurants over the following weeks.

Tim remembers approaching The Emerald on Cup Night, welcomed by the glow of media lights and throngs of people. The replay was shown, the roar sounding bigger than it did for the race itself, the joy recreated.

Phone messages were checked, many emotional, others funny, such as one to Adrian: 'I can't believe that Adi Brown has won more Melbourne Cups than Sheikh Mohammed bin Rashid al Maktoum!'

The joy was shared at that party and in the months following, Sam delighted by the look on people's faces as they had their turn holding the Cup. Even people who had enjoyed the best of racetrack success themselves, such as Black Caviar's owners, who asked if they could have their photo taken with it.

The Cup has been doing the rounds ever since it was won, each owner having a turn with it. It has had many a night out and may, Sam admits, be a little worse for wear. 'It has been handled by so many people, but each mark gives it character, it shows how much it has been loved.'

But where did it all begin for Men In Hats, a name suggested by Tim Ashford, fan of the 'tragic' 1980s hit 'Safety Dance' by Men Without Hats.

'We can go when we want to / The night is young and so am I / And we can dress real neat from our hats to our feet / And surprise 'em with a victory cry.'

Tim had noticed that the group would often wear hats to the

country race meetings they so loved to frequent and, 'Funnily enough,' said Sam, 'the name also resonates as a few of us have no hair!'

In late 2010, opening a bank account and each depositing $5000, the group had the aim of buying shares in a few horses, spending half the money on the initial outlay and the remainder on expenses, happy to let it all roll until the funds ran out.

Sam Brown, Adrian Brown, Greg Williams, Mike Botting, Tim Ashford and Scott Jenke. They did not all know each other at first, but were interconnected in some way. Sam hit it off with Tim when they happened to both be watching Australia play Uruguay in an Edinburgh Pub in 2001.

Sam and Scott went to the same high school, Tim and Greg grew up in the same area, Scott worked with Mike, Adrian and Sam are brothers.

'Adrian wasn't even interested in horse racing,' Sam laughed, 'but we needed his money, so I twisted his arm!'

The others all had a love of racing, of the punt, and a few were members at Caulfield or Flemington. They had mixed backgrounds, Sam a podiatrist, Adrian a television producer, Tim a solutions consultant, Scott a geotechnical engineer, Mike a mining engineer and Greg an IT consultant.

An offhand comment in the lead up to the Melbourne Cup had media reporting that the wives and girlfriends had no knowledge of the syndicate until very recently, but it was not strictly true, rather 'a story which just grew legs'.

Deciding to seek the advice of people in racing they knew, the group met with the likes of Luke Sadler (son of trainer John Sadler) to discuss the benefits and pitfalls of racing horses. Not that it mattered what was said, as their minds were already made up.

'We listened to all the positives and blotted out the negatives,' Tim admitted.

And so they dipped their toes into the water, thinking that a tried horse would be the safest first bet. Where's Wellington was his name. He had won at debut but was not very interested in enhancing his record. And he hardly created a fine impression on his new owners — 'On meeting him for the first time he tried to bite us!'

They had more luck with a couple of tried horses with trainer Luke Oliver, Fine Wine and Makeadreamcometrue both winning provincial races.

'We were so rapt,' Greg recalled, 'we thought that was just the best thing!'

At about that same time the group were taking note of how well trainer Darren Weir was going, and they thought a share in a horse with him was something to aim for. They had noted his great strike rate, hoping they could get a horse to follow around the countryside. 'We thought how great would it be to get a Country Cups horse?!'

And so they had a look at Darren's website, rang and had a chat with his racing manager Jeremy Rogers, who mentioned a few of the horses available.

'But we didn't know anything about yearlings or pedigrees,' Sam said, 'so I did some research and a Pentire colt looked the one. My favourite horse was Rangirangdoo, by the same sire … and he was cheap so it was tick, tick, tick. So I said to the boys that we should be getting into this one.'

With their account funds running low, this horse was to be their final chance, 'a pure last throw at the stumps', so much so that he was often referred to as 'the great hope'.

Ballarat Cup Day 2012 was the day Sam first laid eyes upon their purchase. But it was not love at first sight, Prince Of Penzance in a rather cheeky mood that day — 'I was afraid to go near him; I thought he'd bite my hand off!'

The group admitted they were not all that keen on the name Prince Of Penzance upon first hearing it, but it has certainly grown on them — 'As soon as a horse wins, the name is a good one.'

Many times after a win the Men In Hats crew didn't think it

could get any better. A Flemington victory in their horse's first preparation was celebrated, as was his first stakes victory at Caulfield in February 2014.

And later that year the Moonee Valley Cup on W. S. Cox Plate Day. What a thrill, what a high. Scott Jenke was interviewed on radio RSN's *The Thoroughbred* the next morning, telling listeners of the 'fantastic experience', — one 'very very hard to explain to anyone'.

'It was very exciting watching him flash home, and we even talked about the Melbourne Cup for a few minutes after the race. But Darren said we might set our sights a little lower. It was great to win but we'd been rapt just having a horse running on the day.'

Seeing Prince Of Penzance's name on the list of Melbourne Cup nominations that year was amazing in itself so imagine how much the group appreciated the fact that, twelve months later, he actually made it to the big race.

It was at first not a given, with Prince Of Penzance teetering on the brink of ballot order. 'We were nervous wrecks that week,' Sam recalled, noting that they had spreadsheets outlining every possible scenario, checking horse names against nominations and acceptances and, when realising that the horse's place was assured, joy.

'When that news came through I remember punching the air at work. I was shaking; was this really happening?'

Appreciating just how special it was, they each made the most of the experience. Some went to the Cup Eve parade, a few met for dinner in Federation Square, others went to the Call Of The Card.

As a group they were interviewed by the *Herald Sun*, and they thought that would be the pinnacle … 'We thought that article would be the thing we'd be hanging our hats on for the rest of our lives!' Sam laughed.

Of course the experience became all the more special, especially, said Mike Botting, 'that moment when you realise that your dream has come true … and you want that feeling to last forever.'

'After any win we go nuts,' Sam said, 'but holy crap, this was the Melbourne Cup!'

'I was looking around and seeing the look on everyone else's faces, the enormous shock,' said Greg.

Sam had always joked that one day he'd like to own a 100–1 winner, to do it in the Melbourne Cup … 'That's insane.'

And months later it had not sunk in. Which is not such a bad thing, as the thrill is still raw, still there in the everyday. Such as when the group were at a pub watching one of their less talented horses, despondent when he finished out of the placings. But soon after, the racing station cut to an ad … one featuring Prince Of Penzance winning the Melbourne Cup.

'And suddenly, everything was better.'

Sam laughs at the memory of the first Melbourne Cup he attended (2000, Brew), he and some friends dressing up as Hare Krishnas. 'I would never have guessed I'd be back fifteen years later winning it!'

Chapter Twenty-Eight

ARTHUR RICKARD, JENNY MONKS AND SUSAN CAHILL

As a young boy Arthur Rickard wondered why each Saturday morning his mother, having made scones and tea for the local SP bookmaker, would then sneak off into her bedroom.

On one such morning he decided to follow her. The mystery was solved when he saw his mother draw back the curtains and unpin a piece of paper she had cleverly hidden there.

A list of her day's bets.

Little surprise, then, that Arthur grew up fond of horse racing, and a love of the horse itself was cemented when he began work at the local dairy.

Quitting school the day he turned fourteen, he was offered a job bottling milk and assisting with deliveries. In those days the latter was the job of lovely big Clydesdales, who clip-clopped around Melbourne's streets.

After marrying at twenty-one, Arthur was placed in charge of the Carnegie branch of his company and was pleased to oversee some fourteen horses. And, once it was discovered that he had a knack with them, he was put in charge of procuring horses for other branches across Victoria.

Not far from his home and workplace lived a number of horse racing personalities who would drop by, Arthur looking back fondly on chats with the likes of legendary race callers Bert Bryant and Bill Collins, and the great trainer Angus Armanasco.

After twenty years in the dairy industry, Arthur spent another couple of decades as state manager of Transurety, a company dealing with armoured security vehicles.

Throughout his life remaining close to family members, Arthur enjoyed a particularly good relationship with his brother Keith, who also loved racing.

When Keith first suggested in the early 1980s that Arthur race a horse or two with him, there was no hesitation: 'I jumped right in!'

Racing horses with a variety of trainers, the Rickard brothers enjoyed the occasional winner, Galvaco winning seven races around the bush and one in Adelaide, while Maldive Lad won a couple and was city placed.

Definitely a bit of fun, but not the high life. But Arthur, now in his seventies, had not given up hope of racing a really nice horse.

One day, upon seeing Darren Weir walk past, he called out, 'Hey Weiry, have you got a decent bloody horse for me before I cark it?!'

As it so happened Darren had such a horse, and so Arthur teamed up with his daughters Susan and Jenny, friend Darren Lonsdale and work colleague Mark Hall, and formed the Winning Five syndicate.

One experienced racehorse owner, four first timers.

Not that Jenny is by any means new to horses, after twenty-five years in Prahran moving to Ballarat for the space that country living offered — space for a couple of riding horses and a couple of miniature ponies.

A keen rider when she was young, at sixteen having saved up to buy her first horse — a 3/4 Arab by the name of Tom Thumb — she put horses on the backburner as she married and raised a family.

But the equine passion was always there and, as well as riding her own horses, she takes trips — a trek through Victoria's high country just prior to the Melbourne Cup, with another around Gympie and Noosa planned.

It was her father's involvement with the dairy's Clydesdales that gave birth to Jenny's love of horses. 'My sister and I would ride our favourites around Carnegie, a big black horse called Brandy … and Jack, an ex-pacer.'

Being around horses was, she said, 'a lovely way to grow up'.

And it was at a local riding school that she met her future husband Jody, who was working there on weekends.

At first umming and ahhing when her father asked her to join a syndicate, Jenny thought she'd like to see the horse first. She was pleased he was locally trained — she did not want to be too far away, she wanted to see him race.

She remembers her first meeting with Prince Of Penzance and what stood out most about him — his size, or rather a lack of it.

'He was tiny!' she laughed. But that and the youngster's plainness did not put her off — 'They don't have to be the best lookers to run.'

Taken by his kind eyes, Jenny was also taken by the horse's calmness, something that she still sees in him after he races — 'He doesn't seem to sweat up as much as other horses do; he never looks like he has done it hard.'

Jenny remembers an early conversation with a farrier working on her horses, one who also happened to work for Darren Weir.

He told the story of Prince Of Penzance, as a young horse, waiting to be shod. The horse before him had a meltdown, going down on the ground and kicking wildly. Horses tend to be very responsive to the moods of others — panic begets panic.

But Prince Of Penzance just stood aside, putting himself out of harm's way, barely blinking an eye. The farrier was impressed and so was Jenny.

Melbourne Cup Day, Arthur recalls, was a long one. One which he started off sober, ending up 'legless!'

And of course overjoyed, the thrill of Prince Of Penzance's

victory one he will take to his grave, noting that, 'I now don't have to worry about what there is to say in my obituary.'

He laughs at the memory of the race's immediate aftermath. 'I wouldn't know half the people I spoke to, and there always seemed to be someone shoving a microphone in front of my face.'

Arthur's turn with the Melbourne Cup trophy coincided with Christmas Day, but he didn't tell his family he had it, choosing to instead surprise his daughters on the day by walking in holding it aloft.

Some Santa Claus, that one!

The Cup accompanied Arthur to his usual haunts, including his barber in Keilor Road, Niddrie and nearby Sam's Cafe. The congratulations continued and Jenny received plenty at work, hearing from colleagues across the state to whom she had rarely even spoken.

'There were a lot of people who'd had their first ever bet on him and they just wanted to thank me!'

Catching up with relatives over the following months, Arthur was regaled with many a story of those who had backed Prince Of Penzance, one who'd won $35,000 on the trifecta having heard him mentioned on radio, while another had a nice each-way bet — 'Mainly because her dog's name was Prince and her favourite number was nineteen!'

Arthur's enjoyment of and appreciation for his great horse is heightened by the time he has spent with him. He was a regular visitor when Prince Of Penzance was recovering from his operations, and loves nothing more than to pop into the stables and 'just poke around the horses'.

Jenny remembers one particular visit when Prince Of Penzance was spelling after his Cup triumph. A head collar was ready to lead the horse to his owners, but it wasn't needed. He just wandered over to them, dropping his head right down to his knees so that they could scratch his ears.

It was, Jenny recalls, 'just lovely'.

Chapter Twenty-Nine

DARREN LONSDALE

TO soothe his nerves on the days on which his horse Prince Of Penzance is due to race, Darren Lonsdale takes his dog Jack out for a morning stroll.

On the morning of the 2015 Melbourne Cup, Jack needed a bit of extra puff, as his excited owner had a few more nerves than usual to walk off.

For the most part, that Tuesday was like any other race day. Darren and his wife Amanda, with their daughter Emily and her boyfriend Cameron, boarded a train to Flemington, chatting as they normally would, checking their phones.

The massive crowds at Flemington ensured that it was not such a normal race day, but the Lonsdale family found a spot in the members grandstand and whiled away the first few hours with a little bet here, a little bet there.

And before they knew it, race six had been run and won by Don't Doubt Mamma and it was time to head to the mounting yard.

Limited tickets had been issued so not everyone could get in, but Darren was there and, determined to preserve each exciting moment, he had his mobile phone on, recording it all.

People everywhere, groups of owners huddled in conversation with their trainers and jockeys, the same look of tense anticipation on every face.

Except for one person. Michelle Payne, who was remarkably cool, notably composed. It was almost as though she knew … though, of course, nobody could.

Darren remained in the mounting yard for the running of the race, Amanda and Emily in the crowd. It was hard to see much so Emily held her phone up high and pressed record, at the same time holding onto her lucky charm, a bit of Prince Of Penzance's hair that she had taken to all of his races.

Like the others they were quiet during the race, vocal at the finish. In the yard Darren was one of a big group embracing and making plenty of noise — 'It was crazy, we were jumping up and down and yelling, "Go Pop!"'

'A goosebumpy moment,' is how Emily described it. 'I screamed and jumped and hugged Mum and Cameron. I remember overhearing some young boys behind us say, "Do you think they backed that horse?" Little did they know!'

It's a moment almost frozen in time. 'Every time we watch the race, hear it or even think about it we just get those goosebumps all over again,' said Emily.

'It was seven months ago,' Darren added, 'and I still remember everything so clearly, it feels like yesterday.'

For every owner of the thoroughbred the Melbourne Cup is the pinnacle. It is achieved only by the few, and most of those after they have raced many horses, some good, some slow.

For Darren Lonsdale, however, Cup success came quickly.

With his very first horse, in fact.

'I had no right to go straight to the top,' he admits, but he is pretty happy to be there!

Like his father Les, Darren had been an interested observer of racing for years, enjoying the occasional day out at the track and a bit of a punt.

He was at the races with his friend Arthur Rickard on that fateful day, when a quick yell out to a passing Darren Weir resulted in his first plunge into racehorse ownership, something that had always been in the back of his mind.

'But I had just always assumed it would be too expensive.'

In an age of syndicates, of big groups of friends and strangers getting together to race a horse, the sport has become more affordable to a wider group of people than ever before.

And so Darren laid out a modest sum for a small share — 'The best $1000 I've ever spent.'

'The key thing for me,' he recalled, 'was that Darren said if the horse was no good he'd give us another one. That practically guaranteed we'd get at least a reasonable horse.'

And from the second Darren signed up he became 'obsessed'. He was there for Prince Of Penzance's first trials and his first race at Stawell in March 2013.

'It has been an unbelievable journey,' he said, recalling the first time Michelle Payne hopped aboard the bay in a trial at Colac. 'Darren Weir asked her if she knew much about the Pentire breed, and another jockey overheard and said, "They make great jumpers." I must admit, I was annoyed; I took it personally!'

But affront soon turned to pride as Prince Of Penzance showed the first glimpse of what he had to offer.

'Coming around the turn he slipped, and Michelle's knee nearly hit the ground. He just picked himself up and took off. Michelle got off and said, "No horse does that." She told me that we were going to have a lot of fun with this horse. I just thought she was being nice, keeping me happy. But she knew.'

Start number one and it was just Darren (who had also travelled all the way from Melbourne to Camperdown and Terang for trials) and John Richards cheering. 'First horse, first run, first win. I could not believe it. I celebrated liked I'd won the Melbourne Cup!'

While Darren was hooked from the start, immediately bonding with a horse who he says he often talks to and gets a response from, it took a little while for Amanda and Emily to come around. Not too long, though, for they were at Flemington when Prince Of Penzance recorded his first metropolitan victory in May 2013.

An elderly man on a Flemington gate must have had some sort of premonition that day for he approached Darren, asking him if Prince Of Penzance was his horse and saying, 'You've got yourself a Melbourne Cup horse.'

Fast forward a couple of years and the Lonsdale family's love for Prince Of Penzance is well and truly cemented. They all adored him before the Melbourne Cup. And now they idolise him.

Within a couple of days of the Melbourne Cup, Emily had set up a Facebook page in tribute. She was amazed by the response — 'Within twenty-four hours there were a thousand members from all around the world.'

Darren didn't feel much up to work after the race, so he texted his boss on the Wednesday asking, 'Do you reckon you can cover me for the rest of the week?'

His boss responded, 'Take as much time as you want, everyone is pretty happy for you here.'

It would be three weeks until Darren returned to work at the Austin Hospital, and what a welcome he received. 'I have never had so many hugs and kisses from so many ladies!'

Darren had dabbled a little on the punt, putting $25 each-way on at 150–1 early and a few more little bets here and there — and his co-workers had placed sentimental bets in support, making him a very popular man indeed!

Especially with one particular lucky fellow, whose $1500 each-way netted him in excess of $130,000.

'The win really boosted morale in our area,' said Darren. 'Everyone was so excited.'

And all the more so when it was Darren's turn to look after the Cup for a couple of days. It was dropped off by another owner at the Austin and it did the rounds, many a happy snap taken.

The Cup Night celebrations were long and strenuous at The

Emerald and the casino. Darren didn't arrive home till 5am, but sleep was not really on the agenda. Which was lucky, as the phone rang just a few hours later, a Perth radio station keen for an interview.

'It was hilarious,' Emily recalled, 'he barely had a voice, he was so husky!'

A get-together at the All Nations Hotel in Richmond took place the following day, and the parties just kept happening. There were more celebrations during a family trip to Fiji, where they were surprised by local support. 'Everyone knew about Prince Of Penzance. They'd backed him and were keen to talk about the lady jockey,' Darren laughed.

On 16 January at yet another function, coincidentally on Darren's birthday, with Michelle Payne in St Kilda, the family enjoyed 'special time' with their favourite jockey.

'We watched the race again and asked Michelle to put her hand up when she thought she had the race won. It went up at the 600-metre mark.'

Other members of the Lonsdale family have relished the Cup victory as well, such as Amanda's mother Joyce Ennis, who lives at the Corangamarah nursing home in Colac. Here every resident is now an unabashed Prince Of Penzance fanatic.

One of them even took the time to knit a couple of Prince Of Penzance bears, donned in the silks, with whip in paw. Emily has one, Michelle the other.

There's not a day goes by that Darren doesn't think and talk about the Melbourne Cup. And to go with the photographs, videos and memories, the Lonsdales also have something else, something so precious that it is transported in its own suitcase.

Made by Craig Bannan, a relative who just happens to be a talented silversmith, it is a gold-plated full-sized replica of the 2015 Melbourne Cup trophy.

Chapter Thirty

MARK HALL

FROM novice to enthusiast, the racing journey of Mark Hall.

Not only had Mark never before owned a horse, he had never even thought about it. He was neither a racegoer nor a punter.

His only family connection with horse racing was his father who, as a young man, had for a time worked as an SP bookmaker — on Saturday nights travelling to a city pub to settle bets.

Mark looks back at that era with amazement, recalling stories of high-profile police officers known simply as a Mr Smith or a Mr Jones, who would not only turn a blind eye but who would be betting themselves.

Fast forward decades, and when friend Arthur Rickard 'out of the blue' mentioned that he was putting together a syndicate, Mark thought why not?

He didn't at first inform his wife Fiona of his decision, and it was not until she noticed $25 disappearing each week that the truth was revealed.

Fiona, who works at a bank, was alarmed, worried that someone had hacked their account. She was preparing to ring and have it sorted out.

'You better not do that,' Mark said, rather sheepishly. But there were no dramas; Fiona wasn't fussed. And now she and the whole family are enjoying the Prince Of Penzance ride.

Mark couldn't make it to the track for Prince Of Penzance's debut in March 2013, but watched the race from a Keilor TAB with Arthur. He had no expectations, thinking he'd just see what happened.

Being a first-time owner, he didn't realise what a rush winning was. But it hit him hard and quickly. It didn't take Prince Of Penzance long to turn this owner into a regular at the track.

Prince Of Penzance's third start, his two-length victory at Ballarat, and Mark was there. His first taste of the winning owners' room and he still remembers enjoying a can of Carlton Draught and a party pie.

Already mad keen racing fans, Alan and Ann Burgess started to join in the fun. They have joined their friends Mark and Fiona at many a race meeting, from Mornington and Ballarat to Morphettville. 'We refer to them as the non-financial owners of Prince Of Penzance,' Mark joked.

And he is delighted that there are many such fans of his horse. Each time an owner celebrates a win there is a flow on. Family, friends, and friends of friends also rejoice.

As do Mark and Fiona's children, Emily, Lachlan and Liam. The latter has especially embraced horse racing, and cherishes a photo of himself and Stevie Payne taken in the Flemington mounting yard after the big race.

Admitting that he suffers from a rather severe case of nerves prior to each race, Fiona telling him that he is hard to be around, Mark was on edge well before the Melbourne Cup was due to kick off.

It was difficult to sit still so he wandered around the course, visiting Prince Of Penzance in his stall, strolling through the crowded betting ring, having a last-minute dabble on the punt.

Mark and his fellow owners had found it difficult to secure enough tickets to get into the mounting yard but still they managed, admitting that Fiona ducked in when gate staff briefly glanced the other way.

Once in there, he decided, he would not risk leaving and so watched the race from ground level, not seeing a lot but able to judge Prince Of Penzance's progress from the reaction of those around him.

'I started to notice other owners getting pretty excited,' he said, 'and the rest is history.'

As he embraced the mayhem with everyone else, Mark was amazed and amused to suddenly find himself 'semi-famous'.

'There was a lot of media, everyone wanting to get a minute grab here and there.'

And not just on course, Mark's phone ringing as a radio commentator requested a live interview. 'I have no idea who he was or even how he got my number!' he laughed.

The winner's room and then committee room celebrations ensued, Mark pleasantly taken aback by the hospitality shown to them. 'It was quite astonishing as there were so many of us, and we were allowed to bring all our hangers-on in as well.'

Next up, after cheekily jumping the lengthy taxi queue, the Halls headed to The Emerald. The next day was a quiet one as 'we just let it all wash over us'.

On the following Friday, enjoying a night out at the local football club where Liam plays, Mark and Fiona found themselves the centre of attention. 'We could not pay for a drink, and everyone wanted to hear our story.'

A get-together of family and friends at the Hall home was also fun, Mark replaying the barrier draw vision and the race, before bringing in a surprise guest, the Melbourne Cup itself.

A few months later Fiona and a friend were in New Zealand and, upon realising that she was not far from Prince Of Penzance's birthplace, she gave his breeders a ring to see if she could visit.

Driving past a 'Rich Hill Stud, breeders of the 2015 Melbourne

Cup winner Prince Of Penzance' sign she was warmly welcomed, enjoying a full tour of the farm and getting to meet Prince Of Penzance's sire, Pentire.

On Australian Guineas Day in March, Mark was excited when the Darren Weir trained Palentino, part owned by friends, won the feature race. And so he rushed to the mounting yard, allowed in just by saying, 'I am one of Prince Of Penzance's owners!'

Since the Melbourne Cup, Mark has changed careers. It had been the intention for a while, but the prize money made the transition a smoother, less stressful one.

And winnings have also enabled him to buy shares in other horses, though he knows striking gold again is unlikely. It was something he learned quickly when Megabite, who had taken eighteen months just to get to the track after a series of setbacks, debuted at Kyneton just a couple of weeks before Prince Of Penzance saluted at Flemington.

Misbehaving in the mounting yard and at the gates, the four-year-old also put on a show in the race, buck-jumping and in the process injuring a tendon, his racing career over in an instant.

No doubt horse racing is a game of lows and, for the lucky ones, considerable highs.

Chapter Thirty-One

WILAWL GO RACING

DAVID Wood and Jack Laws were best mates, lifelong friends. They went to school together, they went to work together, they went to war together.

And in November 2015, their families toasted their memories in the best way possible — with a Melbourne Cup.

Wilawl Go Racing, part-owners of Prince Of Penzance. A tight group of family and friends consisting of David Wood's daughter Pam Wilson, her husband David and their sons Andrew, Stephen and Michael. And Jack Laws' sons Neil and Ken.

A part of each other's lives for as long as they can all remember. And all of them horse racing fans, for years getting together on Melbourne Cup Day for a barbeque and a bet.

It seems strange to them that their usual Cup Day celebrations did not take place last year, almost as though the 2015 Melbourne Cup didn't happen.

They were not at the Laws family farm at Gisborne as they usually were on that famous November Tuesday. The usual casual, laidback afternoon was replaced by a frantic, busy, nerve-racking, exhilarating day at Flemington.

It is, of course, every racehorse owner's dream to have a Melbourne Cup runner. But the Wilawl team never imagined it would happen to them. So when it did they were determined to make the most of every moment, and to enjoy it together.

So syndicate manager Pam booked a couple of apartments at Docklands, and on Cup Eve they wined and dined, 'celebrating having a horse in the Melbourne Cup.'

'We thought that was going to be our big night,' she laughed.

While they suffered from pre-race day nerves, the group didn't have too much trouble sleeping that night. They were, said Michael, 'already exhausted from having thought about the race so much!'

On their balcony watching fellow guests spill onto the pavement in all their race day finery, it started to sink in what was happening. It was hard to believe, Pam recalling that, 'Those people were getting dressed up to go to the races and they would be watching our horse.'

Leaving for Flemington so early that they avoided the usual traffic snarls, the families were on edge on course, not sure what to do with themselves. So they wandered around a bit, more often than not ending up at Prince Of Penzance's stall.

Which happened to be box nineteen, the same number as his Melbourne Cup saddlecloth. An omen, surely?

Another omen in a run of omens. A couple of weeks previously, entering Hamilton racetrack where they had a runner, Andrew spotted a horseshoe on the ground, returning to his car to place it under his seat as a lucky charm.

Arriving on course, David found a $10 note on the ground. Sitting on a bench in the mounting yard before the race, he was the recipient of bird droppings on his shoulder. Oh, and their horse, Leica Day, won.

Entering Flemington's gates, David found another $10 note on the ground. Things were looking good!

Huddled around Michelle Payne as she discussed tactics, Prince Of Penzance's owners listened in awed silence. They didn't quite know what to say, the usual good luck seemed somewhat inadequate for such a momentous occasion.

But Andrew found just the right words: 'Go out there and have fun!'

The race seemed, said Michael, 'to last forever'. For a while it was a race of little change, as is the norm in staying races. Prince Of Penzance had dropped his head, a sure sign of a happy, relaxed horse.

Approaching the straight, the Wilawl group realised their horse was now more than the top ten chance they'd been told to expect. And when he hooked out into the clear …

'Everyone just went crazy,' said Andrew.

Well, except Andrew, who was so overcome by it all that for a few seconds he lost his vision, stepping back as though about to faint, before regaining his balance and punching the air.

'It was electric,' said David, 'an unbelievable feeling.'

'We were all crying and I had yelled that much I lost my voice,' Andrew said, while Michael was a bit at sea, having lost his glasses in the mayhem. They were handed to him by a stranger — 'I have no idea who he was but I gave him a great big hug!'

He can't quite remember how he got there, but Neil found himself out in the yard as Prince Of Penzance returned, proudly keeping stride with his horse as the well-wishers honed in.

Stephen, who in his role as General Manager of Communications for the AFL Gold Coast Suns, was familiar with many of the journalists in the mounting yard. He remembers joking with the *Herald Sun*'s Daryl Timms before the race about his job of interviewing the winning owners.

'And there he was after the race, a big grin on his face.'

Soon they were up on the presentation stage, where Michael — possibly the youngest ever owner of a Melbourne Cup winner — was again feeling a little worse for wear.

'I thought I was going to faint up there. I was the first person in the owners' room, looking for some panadols.'

As others headed up to the committee room to continue the

celebrations, Michael found himself some nice cool face washers and a quiet spot to reflect … the toilet!

Once composed he headed out, only to run into Neil having a chat with former Victorian Premier Denis Napthine. 'I couldn't handle it all yet, so I went back and sat on the loo for another ten minutes.'

A big night at The Emerald ensued, the Wilawl families the last to leave at just before 3am. It was a fun night, one they didn't want to end. All the more enjoyable for having been unplanned.

Back to Docklands and not much sleep was had, Neil recalling that he tried to retire just after 3am but was up again at 5am. It was a happy breakfast that morning, one during which they could reflect upon the journey that took them to Melbourne Cup success.

One that began with Pam's father David Wood, a bookmaker. Some of Pam's fondest childhood memories centre around racetracks, where she would run around checking out the odds for her dad, where she would sit on the fence as the horses paraded, her face becoming well known to all the jockeys.

Pam inherited her father's love of horse racing and passed it on to her sons, Stephen recalling doing the form and watching races with his grandfather, who on Saturday nights always had ABC news on for the quadrella leg replays.

The Wilson family always looked forward to visiting the Laws' farm, the boys riding the donkeys, collecting chicken eggs, and feeding the cows and horses. Neil and Ken bred a racehorse here and there, and the families would venture to the races together.

It was only natural that they would all race horses together.

It was six months, however, from that idea to the reality. If they were to have a syndicate everyone was to be involved, and Michael was only seventeen at the time. So they waited, and while many can't wait to turn eighteen to get their driver's licence, for Michael the significance of his birthday was his legal right to own a racehorse.

It was not a fairytale beginning to the Wilawl experience, their very first runner finishing last — 'a terrible, terrible run!'

But quite a fateful last it was, as aboard their not-so-fast horse that day was Michelle Payne.

It was not all doom and gloom, the group sharing a few wins here and there, Tiger By The Tail one favourite. They met several different jockeys, their horses also ridden by Cathy and Maree Payne.

And at that time Neil was employed by Racing Victoria as a financial management teacher at the apprentice jockey's school. One of his charges was a young Michelle Payne, who he remembers being a 'a quiet, driven student who worked hard'.

It was when searching for a new trainer that the Wilson boys noticed how well the up-and-coming Darren Weir was doing. A visit to his stable was organised and a home-bred horse was placed under his care.

Unfortunately, Our Lucky Devil, described by Ken as 'a monster of a horse who liked to unlock his gate and eat all the feed', didn't have what it takes. Nor did their next attempt, the amusingly named Wilawl Avachardy (say that out loud).

It was at about that time, ten years ago, that Darren Weir suggested to them that they would be better off buying ten percent shares in a few horses rather than putting all their eggs into one basket.

It's fair to say that they have had a good bit of fun heeding that advice. Leica Day has won six races, and there have been other winners. But the luckiest day they had was when Darren Weir offered them a share in a Pentire colt from New Zealand.

First impressions of Prince Of Penzance were not exactly favourable, the group visiting the stables to inspect their newest acquisition and finding him lying down cast, or stuck, in his box.

'We'd got up at 5am to drive all the way to Ballarat to see him and there he was, lying down,' David laughed.

'We wondered what we had gotten ourselves into,' joked Ken, 'a horse too dumb to know how to stand up — we've lost our $5000!'

Yell at him, was a stable hand's advice. And so David did, so loudly that his co-owners all jumped up and, thankfully, so did the horse.

And he has been up and running ever since, with the months since his Melbourne Cup victory a whirlwind for Wilawl syndicate members, who have enjoyed many a celebration.

The day after the race they headed to Ballarat to visit their champ, and the signs of the previous night's stable party were clearly visible, one staff member's blackened feet stuck out from under a pile of newspapers, Darren Weir's trophy sitting among scattered pizza boxes.

It was back to Ballarat for the Prince Of Penzance reception, everyone amazed with the turnout.

Shortly afterwards, David took a bit of time out and went fishing — 'I couldn't stand the pace!' he joked.

When returning to work at the Gold Coast Suns, Stephen was confronted by walls plastered with the front page of the *Gold Coast Bulletin* — a photo of himself with Darren Weir. It was, he joked, 'the only newspaper the day after the Cup without a picture of Michelle on the front!'

When it was Stephen's turn to have the Cup trophy, he took it to the club, each of the players keen to have their turn sharing the glory.

A staff member's wife was suffering from bowel cancer and a charity cricket match was held, funds raised by charging attendees to have their photo taken with the Cup.

A function for family and friends was held at Bell's Hotel in South Melbourne, with 150 people showing up. 'I thought we'd only invited ten or so people each,' said Neil, 'but there were people everywhere!'

In January, realising that they didn't have many photos from Cup Day, they returned to Flemington with a photographer, posing in race day clothes, holding their trophy in the mounting yard and on the track in front of the finishing line.

The Cup has also been to the schools where Pam, Neil and Ken teach, and in June Andrew took it to Ringwood Heights Primary where a friend works. The kids were 'euphoric' in response to the trophy, taking turns touching it while firing out questions, such as, 'Does Prince Of Penzance live in your backyard?'

One Grade 4 lad, Jai, already a racing fanatic, had once told his teachers that his dad rode Makybe Diva. He listened carefully to everything Andrew said, then followed him around the school, taking the Cup from classroom to classroom and giving his own little speech each time.

So where does Wilawl Go Racing go from here? They know they have beaten the odds, as Ken said, 'Somebody wins Tattslotto every Saturday, the Melbourne Cup is only won once a year.' They have reached the pinnacle.

But at the heart of things for them it is 'all about the horses.' They will continue to travel to race meetings near and far (that lucky horseshoe still under Andrew's car seat) and they will keep cheering.

'It doesn't matter if it's Donald or Flemington,' said Neil, 'we will yell and scream and look silly.'

Chapter Thirty-Two

ANDREW BROADFOOT

WINNING the Melbourne Cup is such a shock, such a surprise, that a lucky owner may not at first believe that it has actually happened.

Especially if, buried up in the back of Flemington's oldest grandstand from where members have watched Melbourne Cups since Backwood's success in 1924, their view is not the best.

That is where Andrew and Kim Broadfoot and their children, Molly, Alice and Sapphire, ended up watching the 2015 Melbourne Cup.

Andrew and Kim had been keen for their daughters to make the most of the Melbourne Cup, getting to the mounting yard early in order to secure a place on the fence to witness the unfolding of pre-race festivities.

'We thought that would be the highlight of the day,' Andrew laughed.

From there they watched as twenty-four jockeys from around the world were introduced to 101,015 racegoers. Michelle Payne received probably the loudest, most enthusiastic applause. From the crowd and from the Broadfoots.

There was further ovation as Nadia Aya, replacement for late scratching Jessica Mauboy, belted out the national anthem.

Then a flurry of activity as trainers gave last-second instructions to jockeys as they mounted their horses. It is a brightly coloured spectacle before every race, but with a big field on a sunny day it is all the more so.

With the stairs leading to the grandstand being situated at the back of the yard, the Broadfoot family were among the last to get through the scrum, by which time the good viewing spots were taken.

Andrew and Kim were at the back, behind the television cameras and next to a pillar that severely impeded their view. The girls sat on the concrete steps, the youngest Sapphire — as three-year-olds are prone to do — wanting to explore and wander.

And so as the Melbourne Cup was run Andrew had one eye on the race, the other on his daughter. It was not easy to concentrate, a task made all the more difficult by the fact that Andrew is blue-and-green colourblind.

This made picking out Prince Of Penzance's dark green sleeves and cap tricky. He had him in sight for some of the race, losing him at other stages.

And so he was not completely certain that it was his horse hitting the lead, even though Kim was telling him it was so.

But could it be? Was that just too good to be true?

He could see the finishing line — it looked like Prince Of Penzance, but was it?

'I couldn't believe what I thought I'd seen!'

There was 'absolute silence' in the owner's seating area as the horses crossed the line, and Andrew wondered … it must be a long shot, a horse nobody here is cheering. He knew his fellow owners were all watching from the yard.

He turned to a nearby spectator and asked … who won? It was a pretty good answer, and Andrew well and truly enjoyed his walk down the stairs and back to the mounting yard.

Despite being told that there would not be enough room for

his family on the presentation stage they still made it up there, Sapphire amusing herself by sliding down the hand rail. She and her sisters were handed Emirates hats and thought the whole thing was 'pretty special'.

The following days were exciting, Andrew recalling that it was difficult to concentrate once he returned to work — 'I think I was pretty distracted for a while!'

Prince Of Penzance is just Andrew's second foray into racehorse ownership, with his first, from the debut crop of champion stallion Redoute's Choice, managing an Echuca sixth as his best effort.

'It was pretty frustrating watching others of the breed win Golden Slippers and Blue Diamonds,' he laughed, 'and I said, "Never again."'

Racing horses is the ultimate gamble and Andrew was never a big punter — 'It would take a long time to lose that sort of money having a bet!'

But colleague and friend Patrick Wheelahan had enjoyed more luck, racing the Darren Weir trained Geelong Cup winner Leica Ding, who finished fourteenth in the 2009 Melbourne Cup won by Shocking.

And so Darren Weir was always on the radar. It was while exploring the trainer's website one day that Andrew noticed for sale a colt by Pentire.

Andrew was a fan of the breed, especially of the multiple stakes winner Pentastic, who had acquitted himself well in two Melbourne Cups, finishing fifth to Media Puzzle in 2002 and fourth behind stablemate Makybe Diva the following year.

'I knew the Pentire breed had a pretty good record of at least getting to the track,' Andrew said, at the time noting that the advertised yearling was out of a Mr Prospector mare, the same cross that had produced Pentastic.

Making up his mind to take ten percent, thinking he'd be happy to get a horse capable of winning at Stawell or Edenhope, Andrew rang Jeremy Rogers at the stable.

Alas there was just five percent left. Jeremy offered him a ten percent share in any of the other horses advertised on the site, but he decided, most fortunately, to go with his gut and stick with his first selection.

And then there was the waiting game that is horse ownership. It is a test of patience at the best of times, all the more so with a slow maturing staying type.

'But from that first race we could see that he was going to be a better than average horse.'

Ever since then Andrew has attempted to be at as many of Prince Of Penzance's runs as commitments will allow. He has enjoyed watching his family embrace the experience … which is why he was so keen to have his daughters with him on Melbourne Cup Day.

It was quite demanding, the long day and the big crowd proving quite draining on them. By the time the Cup was run, he said, 'they were sick of it!'

As happy enjoying a day out at Ballarat races as they are at Flemington, the girls did, however, enjoy the post-race Melbourne Cup celebrations. They were quite impressed by the committee room, where they were waited on, sausage rolls and sandwiches brought to them.

And the occasion was captured by a photo of the whole family in the yard after the race, a picture they will 'cherish forever'. As will a couple of treasures found by Alice in the backyard on Melbourne Cup eve: two four-leaf clovers. The omen of a lifetime.

Intending to enjoy a quiet Cup Night dinner, Andrew and Kim had already organised babysitters. But they were happy to change their plans, after dropping the kids at home heading with the throng to The Emerald Hotel.

When it was their turn to have the Melbourne Cup, the girls took it to school for show-and-tell. It also spent a day with Andrew at work, and for a couple of weeks it sat on the kitchen bench at the family home.

Andrew is delighted that the Cup has been near and far — 'It has been so nice to share it around, so many people get a lot of pleasure out of it.'

And for the Broadfoots hopefully there is more to come, as Andrew has purchased shares in both of Prince Of Penzance's younger siblings with the Henry Dwyer stable.

Three-year-old filly Penthouse Princess has had a couple of starts and, typical of the breed, needs time. Meanwhile, the final foal produced by Royal Successor has begun his education.

Andrew also has a few shares in other horses with the Darren Weir stable, noting that Prince Of Penzance 'has funded all the others'.

Andrew's newest pride and joy is a boat he is building to enjoy a long-held fishing hobby. Will it be called Prince Of Penzance? Not quite, but it will be named in honour of him … *The Longshot*.

Chapter Thirty-Three

A TRIBUTE

NO story of the Melbourne Cup is complete without mention of the gallant Red Cadeaux.

For five consecutive years the baldy faced chestnut made the long trek from his stables at Newmarket, England, to Flemington.

It was in 2011 that he first came to the attention of Australian racegoers, the Ed Dunlop trained gelding earning his place in the Melbourne Cup field courtesy of a nine-length victory in the Curragh Cup five months previously.

'The Melbourne Cup could be just the right type of race,' Ed Dunlop said at the time, 'and I think we would have a lot of fun out there.'

Despite his good lead up form including a third in the Irish St Leger, Red Cadeaux was big odds come Cup Day. And he went oh so close, in a thrilling neck and neck drive to the line only just pipped by Dunaden.

Twelve months later, having won the Yorkshire Cup, he was back. But his task from barrier eighteen was a tough one. After getting well back, spotting the leaders some fourteen lengths, he was game to the line, finishing eighth after twice striking trouble.

By the time Red Cadeaux, then seven, was back in Melbourne in 2013, he had successfully campaigned in another six countries, winning the prestigious Hong Kong Vase and running game placings in the Dubai World Cup at Meydan and the Tenno Sho at Kyoto.

Despite this he was 60–1 in a Melbourne Cup where much of the attention was on the favourite, the Gai Waterhouse trained Fiorente.

With Gerald Mosse aboard he enjoyed a nice run midfield, hitting the lead in the straight. But Fiorente was too strong. Another photo finish second.

Before heading home Red Cadeaux again raced in Hong Kong, Dubai and Japan. Everywhere he went he was appreciated and adored. Racing fans love a warrior.

Nowhere was he more idolised than in Australia. And that admiration grew all the more with his run in the 2014 Melbourne Cup. Once again he hit the lead, once again another horse finished that bit better, this time Protectionist.

The following autumn Australians had another chance to cheer on Red Cadeaux, this time at weight-for-age level. He ran at Flemington, fifth in the Australian Cup won by Spillway, and at Randwick, second to Criterion in the Queen Elizabeth II Stakes, finishing off strongly after being blocked for runs at a vital stage.

As he strolled around the birdcage prior to the running of the 2015 Melbourne Cup, Red Cadeaux looked calm and well, his bright chestnut coat gleaming. He was one of the most photographed horses by fans.

'It is fabulous,' Ed Dunlop's travelling head lad, Robin Trevor-Jones, tells Channel 7, 'the support he gets, the way Australians have taken him on board.'

History says that Red Cadeaux did not complete the course that day. As Prince Of Penzance was making his winning run, the brave traveller faltered. Gerald Mosse was quickly off.

His horse had fractured a bone in his fetlock. The dreaded green screens were erected.

Not everyone in the Flemington crowd knew what had happened. Those who did were in shock, in tears.

But everything possible was being done to save the life of Red Cadeaux. He was transported to the University of Melbourne's Equine Centre at Werribee. Experts from around the world were consulted.

And at first things looked good. It was even announced three days after the race that he was on the mend.

'He is safe, stable and on the road to recovery,' Ed Dunlop reported in his website blog. 'For that, and almost a decade of joyful brilliance, we must be eternally thankful.'

He also paid tribute to Red Cadeaux … 'he's tough, durable and a hardy trier, but he's relaxed enough to travel and a kind horse to boot. He embodies many of the aspects a trainer longs for in his horses, and while he doesn't have a flashy pedigree or wasn't an outstanding yearling, he's proof that quality can come in many forms.'

He thanked the horse's many fans, those 'both at home and in Australia who have latched onto the idiosyncratic magnificence of this horse and elevated his profile into unworldly proportions.'

Sadly, however, thoroughbreds are not great patients, even intelligent, kind ones like Red Cadeaux. The complications arising from the sort of specialised surgery required to pin delicate bones back together are many.

In this case it was blood flow, a lack of it. There was no choice but a heart-breaking one.

On Saturday 21 November, Red Cadeaux was put to sleep.

'My saddest day in racing,' said Ed Dunlop. 'Red Cadeaux has given us and the racing public so much joy, competing with great distinction across the world. He was an incredibly tough competitor with a wonderful nature, and he will be dearly missed by all.'

Three months later the ashes of Red Cadeaux, the highest ever prize money winning British trained thoroughbred, were taken to Flemington. They were placed in the birdcage with a plaque on which there is a brief but moving tribute from his owner Ronald Arculli.

'For a race that stops a nation we were lucky to have a horse who touched a nation.'

Epilogue

2016

'BIGGER, stronger, smarter.'

This is how Maddie Raymond describes the 2016 version of Prince Of Penzance.

On Saturday 21 May, the reigning Melbourne Cup hero had the briefest of autumn campaigns, his owners heading to Adelaide to cheer on their star in the Group Three R. A. Lee Stakes at Morphettville.

The plan was one run and out.

'It was going to be too long from one spring to the next without a run,' Darren Weir explained. 'We wanted to give him a good break after the Cup, have one start, an easy few weeks and start again.'

Starting at double-figure odds in the 1600-metre race, Prince Of Penzance did it tough from the outside draw, sitting wide throughout.

Yet over the final stages of a slowly run race he let fly, charging late. He was only just held off by stablemate Tonopah — another stride or two?

But for now a second was enough. Prince Of Penzance's zest for racing was still present. If anything, it was stronger.

'He's a lot more mature, more settled in himself, more responsive,' Michelle Payne told journalists. 'It's obviously very hard to win one Melbourne Cup, let alone two. But he's a special horse, so who knows.'

Stay tuned.

Acknowledgements

Prince Of Penzance wishes to thank the many people who helped bring his story to print.

Dr Brian Anderson
Luke Archibald
Tim Ashford
Dayne Barry
Sam Beatson
Stephen Bendall
Bill Blakeney
Bobby Borlase
Melissa Boswell-Happ
Mike Botting
Johnno Bower
Chloe Brien
Andrew Broadfoot
Adrian Brown
Barry Brown
Sam Brown
Glenys Buckley
Michael Burn
Susan Cahill
Greg Carpenter
John Castleman
Sharon Chapman
Ellen Yan Cheng
Jack Coffey
Calindy Conway
Bruce Dalton
Joe Dalton
Jonathon Dalton
Sam Davison
Paul Didham
Laura Dixon
Peter Ellis
Briga Fliedner
John Foote
Renee Geelen
Mark Hall
Dean Hawthorne
Patrick Hines
Jo Horton
Sam Hyland
Scott Jenke
Matt Jones
Brian Kelly
Tim Kelly
Tony Kneebone
Paul Langham
Ken Laws
Neil Laws
Michael Leonard
Faye Lewis
Darren Lonsdale
Emily Lonsdale
Nick Lovett
Ashley Lowe
Vin Lowe
Dianne Manning
Max Manning
Joe McGrath
Sandy McGregor
Jarrod McLean
Greg Miles
Jenny Monks
Peter Morganti
David Nagle
Diane Nagle
Terry O'Sullivan
Michelle Payne
Stevie Payne
Lee Purchase
Maddie Raymond
John Richards
Arthur Rickard
Jeremy Rogers
Adam Michael Rumsby
Andrew Seabrook
Robyn Shakespeare
David Tenenbaum
John Thompson
Stuart Trott
Joan Walker
Robbie Waterhouse
Bonnie Weir
Darren Weir
Noelene Weir
Nicholas White
Greg Williams
Andrew Wilson
David Wilson
Michael Wilson
Pam Wilson
Stephen Wilson
Katrina Wood
Warren Wruck

The Author

Ever since seeing the big chestnut Empire Rose overshadow her much smaller rivals in the 1988 Melbourne Cup, Kristen Manning has been well and truly hooked by the magic that is Australia's most famous race.

Dreaming of one day holding her own Melbourne Cup, Kristen has long wanted to write a book about one special winner of the big race, and she is delighted that Prince Of Penzance is that horse.

A journalist specialising in thoroughbred racing and breeding, Kristen has written for a variety of publications, including *Racetrack*, *Bluebloods*, *Winning Post*, *Thoroughbred Racing Commentary* and *Turf Monthly*. She is author of *Fields Of Omagh* (Melbourne Books) and the contributor of four chapters to *Great Thoroughbred Sires Of The World*.